FALLEN FORTRESS

A TRUE STORY OF THE TRAINING AND SURVIVAL OF A DOWNED B-17 PILOT

Tom Bartlett

Pear Tree Press

Published by Pear Tree Press

Copyright © 2014 by Tom Bartlett

ISBN: 978-0-578-15127-4   Printed in the United States of America

Table of Contents

A Note to the Reader

The Army Air Corps was created when it became the branch of Army Aviation in 1926. But in the early 1940s, Secretary of War Henry L. Stimson and Army Chief of Staff George C. Marshall saw the need for a stronger role for Army aviation. So on 20 June 1941, they created the Army Air Force (AAF), formally replacing the old Army Air Corps. The Army Air Forces and the Army Ground Forces were made equal commands. But most of the public and virtually all the press organizations during World War II insisted on calling the aviation arm of our military the "Air Corps." No less authority than Gen. Curtis LeMay commented on the resistance of people to recognize the official change of name: "All through World War II it was 'Our grandson is in the Air Corps,' 'Local Young Man Enlists in Air Corps,' 'And so on.'" Many veterans of the Army Air Force in World War II described themselves as belonging to the "Air Corps." In this book the two terms are used interchangeably.

Chapter 1

The Aviation Cadet

Just prior to the usual 'Bombs Away' a quick sequence of three rounds of anti-aircraft fire slammed into the B-17 that Cornell was piloting. The first round exploded directly into the right hand outboard engine (number four) and virtually blew the engine away in a sheet of flame. Although the engine was destroyed, the wing somehow remained attached. The next round hit near the first, blowing a hole the size of a basketball through the outer wing and gas tank. This tank fed the number three engine. However, for some reason the high-octane gasoline did not ignite. The third hit was either at the open bomb bay doors, or just inside, so the flak must have smashed the bomb release system, making it impossible to drop automatically. Normally, when the bombs left the aircraft, the plane leaped upward as the bombs fell out of the bay. It became clear to the crew that something was jamming the bombs from releasing.

Cornell checked the cockpit and saw that he was bleeding slightly from a shrapnel fragment that hit just above his gloved left hand. Blood from his wrist dripped into the pilot's seat and on some of the controls. This blood evidence would later become very important. Cornell hit the intercom button to ask the crew to check in. While waiting for reports from the crewmembers, he reached over to feather the prop on the number three engine. Combined with the loss of the number four engine, the feathering of the prop on number three meant all the power from the right side of the plane was lost. Cornell pulled the lever to empty the fire extinguishers located in the troubled right wing. He pushed the power to the remaining engines one and two to the upper limit, which caused the left wing to try to climb.

Just seconds away from an uncontrollable spin, Cornell applied the left aileron to lower the wing, at the same time feeding in left rudder to try to offset the loss of thrust from two engines on the right side. He called out to his co-pilot Sullivan to help with pressing on the left rudder pedal. Since all the controls of the B-17 were cable-operated straight from the pedals, it took the combined efforts of both pilots to keep the giant rudder pivoted to the left. The pilot of a B-17 had an emergency manual bomb release in the form of a red ball right beside his left foot. Cornell reached down to pull the release and it came free in his hand. The shrapnel bouncing around in the cockpit must have severed the attaching cable.

The wounded B-17 began to lag behind the rest of the group. The original bombing altitude was eighteen thousand feet and Cornell had to make a series of fast decisions. He had to quickly jettison as much weight as possible and try to stretch his altitude as far as he could. He could not hope to keep up with the safety of the group, so he had to conserve as much of the plane's altitude as he could to try to figure out what to do next. Cornell knew that pushing the two remaining engines to their limit would eventually cause their cylinder head temperatures to climb into the danger zone, but he had no other option. Next he instructed his copilot, Lt. Sullivan, to go back to the bomb bay section to see if the bombs could be released manually. He gave instructions to the crew over the aircraft intercom to dump everything possible overboard, guns, ammo, or anything that was not nailed down. Cornell stood on the left rudder pedal as Sullivan disconnected his oxygen tube, suit heater, and intercom wiring to head back to the bomb bay section. To move about in the plane at this altitude Sully needed to carry along the portable oxygen bottle.

Cornell had no plan except to try to make it back to the English Channel. If they could get that far, he hoped to ditch the plane in the channel close to a boat if possible. One major immediate problem was his missing navigator. His regular navigator, Harry Tennenbaum, had also been trained as an operator for the newly developed radar system. But Harry was not on this flight due to a new policy not to include navigators who had knowledge of the newest radar systems on short missions. All of the other planes had been instructed to follow the lead plane, which contained an experienced navigator. Cornell always remembered Harry standing on the hardstand (parking slot) in semi-darkness as they left without him. Cornell desperately needed continual updates on their position to see if it would be possible to make it back to the channel. Harry would have given him how many minutes he had to go to reach the coast. Harry would have vectored him around some of the hottest anti-aircraft positions. Even flying across the Atlantic and eleven earlier missions over enemy territory, Cornell had delivered the crew safely and they knew their lives depended on his judgement and piloting skills. The crew believed Cornell would get them back alive if he had to personally will the plane to stay in the air. It was this belief that held the crew together and allowed them to act as one.

Years later, Cornell recalled desperately trying to make it back to at least the Channel: *"It had never occurred to me before to ascertain whether all my gang could swim. In Alabama, everyone swims, otherwise they drown. We did wear Mae West life preservers under our parachute harnesses, but they were clumsy affairs when inflated, which would have prevented us from even swimming away from the enemy. On top of this, it was the time of year for heavy swells in the sea, and altogether, prospects for our future well-being seemed grim. Decisions, decisions..."*

*   *   *   *

Rain had been falling for three days without a let-up but still Cornell's Company Commander insisted that the men remain in the field until all the exercises were finished. The swamps outside of Fort Polk Louisiana was the last place on earth the tall reed-thin Pvt. Winans C Shaddix wanted to be stuck while the war continued to rage in Europe and the Pacific. Pvt. Shaddix, or Cornell as he was known to his friends, realized that he could not remember standing on dry ground a single time since he arrived in Louisiana. His boots were muddy, his army fatigues were muddy, his helmet was muddy, his carbine was muddy, he even had mud in his hair and in his ears. It was bad enough to be a lowly Army Private, but to be forced to march and train in the Louisiana mud while his classmates and friends were somewhere overseas carrying the war to the enemy was almost too much for Cornell to bear. He also realized that when his Company finally got back to the barracks it would take hours of cleaning to rid himself, his clothes and his equipment of the ever-present mud.

It seemed like only a few weeks before he had enrolled at the University of Alabama as a freshman intending to major in aeronautical engineering. For all of his young life, Cornell had been fascinated with airplanes and flying. He could still recall the first time he had witnessed the miracle of flight standing with his father at an air show outside Atlanta, Georgia. The sight of two frail biplanes struggling to gain altitude in the hot Georgia sunshine seemed to violate everything that Cornell had learned about gravity in his short life. Standing there in the crowd he vowed one day to be up there in the clouds with the pilots who dared tempt fate and join the eagles in the air. Cornell had enrolled for two night courses in engineering at Georgia Tech but always wanted to study at the University of Alabama. With his father's blessing he transferred to Tuscaloosa, Alabama and started the fall semester. At the same time he also signed up with the local unit of the Alabama National Guard, along with his roommate who was also from Winston County. They did not complete their first semester before their unit was mobilized. So instead of completing his studies at the picturesque campus of the University of Alabama, Cornell found himself undergoing Army maneuvers deep in the swamplands of Louisiana at Fort Polk. To make matters worse, after the events of December 1941 Cornell learned that his unit, the 31st Infantry Division, which was on active duty for a "one-year" mobilization, was extended to the duration of the war. The Division's mission at that time was strictly training; officers and combat personnel underwent maneuvers and practice before being shipped out to the European and Pacific theatres.

The desire to be of more use than just an infantryman, and also to get out of the Louisiana mud were just some of the reasons that Cornell started applying to become an aviation cadet, stressing his background as a student in aeronautical engineering. His father had been an Infantry officer during World War I and maintained a reserve commission afterwards. Cornell had been brought up on tales of war and glory. His forefathers had fought in the Civil War and Cornell had actually met several of the aged veterans when he was just a child.

Once he started the application process, he found it to be lengthy and rigorous, involving not only tests for mathematical skill, mechanical judgement, and leadership qualities, but also for reflexes, coordination, ability to perform under time pressure and visual acuity. A score below excellent in any area would mean instant rejection. Months went by after the testing but Cornell heard nothing. He had almost given up hope until after a particularly trying day on maneuvers he was returning covered in mud with his squad to their barracks when a corporal told him to report to the orderly room. Having no idea what caused this request, Cornell carefully wiped the mud from his boots and checked in with the clerk in charge who soundlessly handed him a set of orders and went about his business. Cornell peered at the mimeographed stack of papers that changed the status of one Pvt. Winans C. Shaddix from infantryman with the 31st Infantry Division to Aviation Cadet Shaddix of Class 43F with the Army Air Corps. No congratulatory letter, no handshake, no slap on the back, just a long set of instructions that set in motion a complex chain of events. The orders directed the Base Financial Section to change Cornell's pay from being a regular enlisted member of the Infantry to that of Aviation Cadet and also to issue a travel voucher from Fort Polk, Louisiana to Santa Ana Army Air Field in Santa Ana, California. Thus his pay went that day from $30.00 per month to $75.00 per month. He felt he was rich.

The Aviation Cadet program really got its start when the United States officially entered the First World War in April 1917. At that time the Army had only three

flying schools, about 125 flyable aircraft, and 96 officers
who had gained flying status. To meet the vastly enlarged
need for more airplanes and pilots, in May 1917 Congress
finally awarded $640,000.00 to improve the status of the
aviation wing of the Army. This amount would fund a
huge expansion in equipment and training for the new
flying weapons. The first training programs were set up in
universities around the country, including the Universities
of California, Texas, Illinois, and Georgia Institute of
Technology, Cornell, Ohio State, and MIT. The program
was patterned after a similar program already in effect in
Canada, including the term "Flying Cadet" for the
students. Although the programs were marked with a
high accident rate and a high percentage of "wash-outs"
the students were awarded a commission as a 2nd
Lieutenant in the Army Reserve if they were able to
successfully complete the course.

After the war ended in 1918 the Flying Cadet
program was sharply curtailed and the university courses
eliminated with most reservists released from active duty.
So to replace the missing aviators, the Army Air Corps
instituted similar programs at Brooks and Kelly Fields in
Texas. Much smaller in number, the training programs
combined physical training, academics, flying training,
and loads of close-order drill. The intensity of the course,
the academic rigor, and the high accident rate all
contributed to reduce the number of graduates. Charles
Lindbergh, a 1925 graduate, remembered that of the 107
students who started with him, only 17 were able to make
it through to graduation. But the Flying Cadet program in
the 1920s and 1930s saw such graduates as Jimmy

Doolittle, Curtis LeMay, Archie J. Old, and Elwood Quesada, all of whom later became generals in the Air Force. In June 1941 with a war appearing more imminent, the Air Corps enlarged the Flying Cadet program and changed the name to the "Aviation Cadet." A year after Pearl Harbor, the Aviation Cadet program had an enrollment of almost 90,000 cadets and reached a high of 109,000 in 1943.

As Cornell was entering Preflight training, most Americans were beginning to adjust to the new rationing rules, which now included shoes, most meats, butter and cooking oils. If gas could be purchased, it normally sold for $.15 per gallon. The military had just completed the world's largest building for its time, the Pentagon in Washington, D.C. In the war abroad, the Germans and Italians had just surrendered their forces in North Africa and General Dwight D. Eisenhower was named the supreme Allied Commander.

Cornell then got to experience his first trip across the continental United States aboard a slow moving troop train: *"It should be pointed out that troop trains of this period were not any slower than say, freight trains. It's just that they had a very low priority in the scheme of traffic routing and some freight trains had an imperative need to be in New Orleans, Brooklyn or some other port to load desperately needed artillery shells, spare engines, or whatever for transshipment to Europe or the Pacific. So we were shuffled off to a siding many times to let a fast moving freight train past."*

Thus Cornell arrived at the Santa Ana Army Air Base in Santa Ana, California. Constructed on 409 acres leased from the city of Santa Ana, the base was hurriedly completed in 1942 and consisted of administrative buildings, cadet barracks, classrooms, cadet-dining halls, a commissary, fire station, chapel, and a 151-bed hospital. The mission of the Air Base was to conduct the initial classification and training of Aviation Cadets and to see if they possessed the qualities deemed necessary to become pilots. Cornell's newest assignment to Preflight training would turn out to be an intensive mixture of enlisted basic training and Officer Candidate School, with a strain of West Point tradition thrown in to make life more interesting. Because of the rapid expansion of flying schools the base was thinly staffed with non-flying officers and sergeants, and so his daily life was closely supervised by the ever-present upperclassmen that were one class ahead of him. In a bow to the West Point tradition, upperclassmen were responsible for the achieving a "military discipline" in the incoming new troops. In this manner the Air Corps could operate with fewer supervisory personnel, with the upperclassmen responsible for the deportment of the incoming troops. They marched the new recruits, yelled at them for the slightest infraction, and required the newcomers to answer all questions in short clipped yells. At any moment an upperclassman could command a recruit to "hit a brace", a sort of exaggerated position of attention in which the body is rigidly posed with shoulders thrown back, chin receded as far a humanly possible, and face locked dead ahead. Although these measures may have or have not worked at West Point, the conditions at a rushed wartime training base were entirely different from a relaxed campus atmosphere. In practice, the use of upperclassmen to inspire discipline in newcomers gave some a chance to simply bully younger recruits and resulted in the almost complete revulsion of the underclassmen to the ones in the class who had arrived just before them.

As a new Aviation Cadet Cornell was initiated into one of the most unusual brackets in the hierarchy of the military--not an enlisted man, although he had enlisted in the Army, but yet not an officer. A cadet was somewhere in between. In his prior experience as an enlisted member of the U.S. Army, Cornell was reminded daily of his status at the very bottom of the military chain of command. To get out of this low position was one of the main reasons he volunteered for flight school. But an Aviation Cadet occupied an indeterminate position in the military chain of command. His instructors were aware of the fact that if he were able to complete the course, he would receive a commission and become an officer. For this reason, and many others, all cadets were addressed as "Mister." It was "Mister Shaddix" regardless if he were being given personal instruction or being chewed out. It seemed to Cornell that some of the Instructors could make the word "Mister" sound like a curse.

At the same time the position of being an Aviation Cadet was extremely tenuous. One failed academic exam and Cornell would be "washed out" of the program and returned to his previous status (and pay) as a foot soldier. Some cadets who passed all their academic courses but yet failed to achieve passable scores on the flying portion were allowed to volunteer to transfer to either Bombardier

School, or if their scores on the math and map reading section were exceptionally good, to Navigator School. In either case if they successfully completed these further courses, they would be commissioned as officers. All others who washed out were usually reassigned for further technical training, but spent the rest of their enlistment as regular enlisted soldiers.

The reality was that every Aviation Cadet was always just on the verge of being dismissed from the Cadet ranks and sent back to the enlisted ranks. Some, like Cornell, adapted to the constant stress and thrived under the pressure. Others did not fare so well. Overall, during World War II nearly 40% of the Aviation Cadets were washed out for one reason or another before the entire program was completed. Even such an occurrence as a sprained ankle, which would not permit Physical Training (PT) every day, or influenza, which could lead to missed classes, could result in a cadet repeating the entire course, or simply being washed out.

Of the many accolades given the United States military services after World War II, perhaps the least attention has been given to the task of educating civilians to become competent soldiers, airmen, and seamen. Many books have been written about the exploits of our courageous soldiers in battle, their sometimes-wise leaders, and the industrial powers that pivoted from manufacturing consumer products to making guns, tanks, and airplanes. But not too many have focused on the enormity of the task of educating the soldiers, airmen, and sailors. General George C. Marshall Army Chief of Staff, was aware of the daunting problems facing him when he inherited in 1939 an Army and Army Air Corps numbering fewer than 200,000 men. When the war ended in 1945, over eight and one-third million men had been inducted, trained, and equipped to wage war. These former civilians became the soldiers who drove tanks, fired artillery shells, and piloted airplanes, in most cases with less than nine months of training.

To accomplish this task of training millions of recruits, the armed services had to adopt the most up-to-date educational practices and put them into effect nationwide. A good example of this training regimen would be the task of training what would eventually total 250,000 civilians to pilot a fighter plane or heavy bomber for the Army Air Corps.

Cornell's pre-flight training was divided into two portions: the first six weeks were devoted to physical training (PT) and introduction to military rules and regulations with copious amounts of close-order drill and marching thrown in. Every Saturday the cadets were required to participate in a huge parade that involved nearly everyone on the base. Cornell had, as a previously enlisted Private, already participated in many of the classes in military rules and regulations, but most of his classmates were entering directly from civilian life or college and needed this introduction to the military. A few of the lessons being covered were new to Cornell, such as the rules of customs and courtesies concerning the conduct of being a commissioned officer. So all cadets were properly introduced to the Army way of doing things, from the proper way to salute to the Army way of making up one's bunk. Cornell excelled in this first introduction to cadet life, partly because of his prior service, and partly because of his great desire to become a pilot and a commissioned officer.

His next three weeks were concerned primarily with academic courses, such as the physics of flight and a refresher in math and physics. Also covered were meteorology, aeronautical map-reading and aerial navigation. Cornell's navigation instructor had been a close friend and associate of Amelia Earhart and Fred Noonan her navigator for her final flight. Cornell stated that the instructor felt that "Noonan was a competent navigator, but one who had an exaggerated opinion of his own infallibility." Cornell passed all his examinations in this first preliminary introduction to the Air Corps so he was one of the ones who were selected to continue on to the actual flying courses, the ones that would be far more demanding, both intellectually and physically.

The standard Air Corps pilot training program was composed of three segments: Primary, Basic, and Advanced. At the beginning of the war three months were devoted to each segment, but as more planes rolled off the assembly lines and more replacement pilots were needed, the segments were shortened to ten weeks and then in 1943 to just nine weeks. Cornell's Cadet class spent nine weeks in each segment

For Primary Flight training Cornell and the cadets were introduced to the basic trainer used by the Army Air Corps in WW2, the two-seat Stearman Kaydet. The airplane, a fabric-covered biplane designed by the Stearman Company, was chosen for its predictable flying qualities and the ruggedness of its radial engine and sturdy airframe. The rugged landing gear in particular saw a difficult life as the student pilots learned how to land and sometimes how not to land. The Air Corps referred to the trainer as the PT-13 (for Primary Trainer). The Stearman Company, which became a subsidiary of the Boeing Company in 1934, produced over 10,000 of these basic trainers. So many Stearmans were built and its flying qualities were so predictable that thousands of army-surplus Stearmans were used as cropdusters after the war

STEARMAN KAYDET PT-13

The student occupied the front cockpit of the PT-13 with the instructor in the rear. Sixty years later Cornell recalled climbing over into the front cockpit and seeing the leather covered seat with the instrument panel full of gauges and the single vertical control stick. The standard method of instruction involved the instructor first explaining the new maneuver, then demonstrating it, with the student then attempting to replicate the maneuver. Any student errors were then corrected and the student would practice the maneuver until he

demonstrated proficiency. The cadets practiced takeoffs
and landings, stalls, climbing and descending turns and
coordinated rolls until their instructor felt comfortable
about allowing them to solo. Then while flying solo the
cadets practiced and mastered more difficult maneuvers
such as crosswind takeoffs and landings, loops, and
elementary aerial navigation. Ground school instruction
consisted of classroom lectures, demonstrations, and then
discussions. Teaching aids such as training films, slides,
and charts were in use constantly. Many classrooms
contained mockups of the cockpit of the plane or the
subject being discussed. Classes were small and everyone
was encouraged to speak up and the instructors made
sure that everyone understood the point being discussed.
The pace was fast and demanding, but every single aspect
of flying and controlling an airplane was thoroughly
covered. Because of the heavy demand for pilots, Cornell's
instructors were civilians recently hired from the airlines.
At the end of Primary Flight training all successful cadets
had completed about 60 hours of flight. Cornell stated
that he thought he was the last member of his class to
solo. But solo he did, and was promoted to the next
phase.

For the next stage, known as Basic Pilot training,
Cornell's cadet class, the ones who had not been washed
out, transferred to Minter Field, about 13 miles northwest
of Bakersfield, California. The field, named for a WW1
airman who was killed in a mid-air collision in 1932, was
typical of the many training bases that were hurriedly
built at the onset of WW2. Hastily built wooden buildings
housed the cadets and classrooms. Larger hangars, also

of wood, provided the space for maintenance shops and equipment. These buildings were all located beside the concrete runways. Officially started in 1941, the base was opened for cadets in 1942. By the time Cornell arrived in 1943, Minter Field was home to some 7,000 military and civilian personnel. Besides the normal barracks, hangars, and classrooms, it was enlarged to include an infirmary, post office, chapel, swimming pool, and theatre. During the war the field would graduate over 11,000 cadets.

VULTEE VALIANT "VIBRATOR"

According to the system then in use by the Air Corps, each training stage entailed mastering a faster, more powerful aircraft. The principle training aircraft at Minter Field was the Consolidated Vultee Valiant, affectionately referred to by the cadets as the "Vultee Vibrator." Several theories were prevalent about how the "Vibrator" gained its name; one attributed it to the plane's shaking as it neared a stall, while another theory ascribed the nickname to the noisy canopy. The students all agreed, however, they could feel the power of the nine-

cylinder radial engine through the airframe. A 450 HP
Pratt & Whitney Wasp R985 engine with a two-stage
propeller powered the plane. The Army Air Corps referred
to the plane as the BT-13 (for Basic Trainer). The trainer
had fixed landing gear and a Hamilton-Standard two
speed prop. It was faster and heavier than the Stearman
that Cornell soloed in and required much more
concentration. It was an all-metal—except for the control
surfaces—monoplane with full instrumentation for night
flying. Cornell mentioned that at the beginning of night
training they were not allowed to leave the local traffic
pattern, but to just make the circuit around the pattern,
practicing landings over and over again. In recalling his
introduction to night flying, Cornell stated,

*"There were few, if any, lights outside the city of
Bakersfield late at night and with any cloud cover it was a
dark and forbidding area with mountains ringing it, except
for the valley to the north. To us young, inexperienced
cadets, it was downright foreboding since we had no visible
horizon to help us keep our wings level and vertigo was
some problem."*

The BT-13's exhaust manifold exited low on the
right side of the plane. While flying at night this exhaust
appeared remarkably similar to flames coming from the
engine. An earlier cadet had become alarmed at this
spectacle and had promptly bailed out of what he thought
to be an airplane on fire. From that day forward, Cornell
recalled, during the student's first night flight the
instructor was sure to say over the interphone:

"Mister, stick your head out over on the right side
of the canopy and look down, are we on fire?"

"Hmm, YES SIR!"

"No, we aren't, that's the exhaust flame, do you understand me?"

Then a subdued, "Yes Sir." End of pointless bailout.

In attempting to turn out competent pilots in such a short time, the Air Corps used every educational tool then available, including spending time in the Link Trainer. The Link Trainer was an early analog version of a flight simulator. Invented and built by Ed Link, the trainer was a staple of flying schools from the late 1930s until the early 1950s, not only in the United States but also in Europe. Link, whose family built organs and nickelodeons in New England, was familiar with pumps, bellows, mechanical levers, and universal joints. As an aspiring pilot, he used his knowledge of these principles to construct in 1929 a flying simulator that resembled a miniature airplane cockpit with shortened wings and fuselage. The simulator would pitch and roll as the pilot worked the controls. The concept was valid but the devices did not find many customers during the years of the depression. However, in 1934 the Army Air Corps took over the Airmail service and shortly afterward suffered a series of devastating losses as their pilots tried to fly in all sorts of inclement weather. In searching for a solution, the Air Corps ordered six of Link's Trainers to acclimate their pilots to instrument flying during bad weather and found the trainers were reasonably effective in teaching pilots to strictly follow their instruments. Pilots who had trained for flying blind on instruments in the Link Trainer had a remarkably lower accident rate than their unlucky predecessors. The time spent in flight simulators was found to be so valuable that updated versions and now all-electronic versions of flight simulators are standard tools in pilot training. The airlines have also found them to be so valuable for transitioning to a new plane that they are a required part of the training. All aviation cadets were expected to spend at least 10 hours in the early simulator. Cornell liked the exercises in the Link Trainer but had a little trouble fitting his tall lanky frame into the small cockpit.

THE LINK TRAINER

As Cornell continued in pilot training, the United States was finally beginning to make progress overseas, both in North Africa and in the Pacific. In the spring of 1943, the United States, who had broken the Japanese secret code, intercepted a message that Admiral Isoroku Yamamoto was planning an inspection trip to Japanese outposts in the Solomon Islands and New Guinea on 18 April 1943. Yamamoto, who planned and led the attack on Pearl Harbor, was the most influential strategist in the

Japanese Navy. Sixteen P-38 fighters were dispatched from Kukum Field on Guadalcanal to make a long over water flight the intercept the Admiral's plane. The Naval Aviators were successful, shooting down both the Admiral's plane and his escort. The loss of Yamamoto was a devastating blow to the Japanese Imperial Navy.

Upon successful completion of Basic Pilot training, yet still an Aviation Cadet, Cornell was transferred to Advanced Pilot training at Yuma Army Air Field, Yuma, Arizona. Another long, hot train ride. Just like Cornell's previous base at Minter Field his new home in Yuma was another Air Corps training base that had been hurriedly converted from a civilian airport to a military training field in 1942. More runways were added and the main ones reinforced for heavier traffic. Wooden barracks, classrooms, maintenance shops, the standard infirmary, and the ubiquitous parade ground for close-order drill were added. For combat training, the Air Corps needed training fields with good weather for all year flying and, more importantly, large open uninhabited areas for target practice. Yuma, Arizona fit the latter criteria exceedingly well.

In keeping with the Air Corps practice of introducing the students to increasingly faster and more powerful airplanes, the next selections were even more advanced. The new planes to master included the AT-6 (for Advanced Trainer) fighter plane trainer, the primarily wooden-structured AT-17 twin-engine trainer, and the all-metal AT-9 twin-engine trainer. The cadets really looked forward to flying the AT-6. Designed by North American Aviation in 1934 as a basic combat trainer, the AT-6 was modified and improved over the years before the war. The plane had a rugged all-metal structure and featured retractable landing gear and both forward and rear facing machine guns. It had all the capabilities, including aerobatics, of a fighter plane except for a limitation in top speed.

AT-6 TEXAN

Experienced fighter pilots found that the plane flew, climbed, dived, and landed similar to their much faster and heavier fighters. In the later 1930s so many improvements to the plane were made that the AT-6 became by 1940 the standard fighter pilot trainer not only for the Air Corps, but also for the Navy (SN-J) and many foreign militaries. Aviation historians believe that from 12,000 to 15,000 of the combat trainer were built before production ended in 1944, with most of the variability coming from the different variations of the trainer being built and some being rebuilt or being updated.

Cornell was introduced to the much faster and more complex AT-6 by first studying the increased number of controls to master. In addition to the usual controls for flaps, trim tabs, and variable pitch propeller, he had to master the controls and procedures for extending and retracting the landing gear and found himself for the first time in a airplane with a fuselage mounted machine gun. The trigger for the gun was located within easy reach at the top of the control stick. With this added complexity was another checklist to memorize, one entitled "*GUMP*":

> **G**-*Gas selector on the fullest tank, fuel pumps on.*
>
> **U**-*Undercarriage (landing gear) down and locked.*
>
> **M**-*Mixture (fuel) control on full (or auto) rich.*
>
> **P**-*Propeller pitch control set for landing (low pitch, high RPM).*

Cadets got their first aerial gunnery practice in the AT-6 and also their first formation flying practice with other AT-6s. After one instance of low-level strafing run at a cloth-and-stick target on the ground, Cornell landed his AT-6 and found two bullet holes in his aluminum propeller. Apparently the synchronizer had failed. Cornell and the other cadets looked forward to lectures from their navigation instructor, Army Air Corps Captain Barry Goldwater, who was a witty and entertaining speaker. Goldwater's self-deprecating humor brightened the long days the cadets putting in. His colorful down-to-earth tips on practical navigation proved to be life saving later for some of the cadets.

Cornell's first introduction to twin-engined aircraft was in the AT-17 built by Cessna Aircraft Company. The plane was a military version of a light transport plane that Cessna had designed to sell to the smaller airlines and charter flight businesses. After the Air Corps purchased several of the earlier versions, it ordered more to use as an advanced twin-engine trainer. Although it had a steel tube frame and was covered in fabric, because it had a wing with a wooden spar and ribs, it was often referred to as the "Bamboo Bomber." Its flying characteristics were predictable and stable thus making it a good multiengine trainer, especially for the introduction to formation flying of multiengine aircraft. Cornell did not realize it at the time, but piloting the twin-engined AT-17 was a good introduction to the multi-engined bombers that he was to fly later.

On the other hand, his introduction to the AT-9, a Curtis-Wright built twin engine trainer, was an entirely different kind of experience. This all-metal twin trainer had been purposely designed to simulate the flying characteristics of a modern heavy bomber and thus was less stable in flight and much more difficult to land. Some pilots, including Cornell, felt that flying a heavy bomber would be good training for attempting to fly the AT-9. He recalled the plane as having "*a glide ratio about like a farm tractor (straight down) when the power was reduced.*" Sure enough, after the war none of the AT-9s were offered for sale in the civilian market.

The cadets got a taste of what parachuting was all about with multiple jumps from a tower, using a static line for control--not actual jumps, just lots of tower jumps and practice landings with a roll. To hopefully improve their target shooting, the cadets were also introduced to skeet shooting and how to "lead" the target.

Meanwhile, the air war in Europe was heating up. For the first time, the 8th Air Force stationed in England was sending bombers deeper into Germany further than their escorts could follow, leaving the bombers to face the German interceptors and anti-aircraft alone. On 11 June 1943 they flew a daylight mission to Wilhelmshaven and Cuxhaven, losing 8 B-17s and suffering damage to another 62 more. On 13 June, in missions to Bremen and Kiel a total of 26 planes were lost. The 8th Air Force commanders were determined to prove that daylight precision bombing could work, so they continued the attacks and began the process of making up the losses in manpower by diverting nearly all pilot trainees into heavy bombers.

So on Tuesday, 22 June 1943, Aviation Cadet Winans Cornell Shaddix along with the ones who remained in Class 43F graduated, were commissioned as 2nd Lieutenants and awarded the coveted Pilot's wings. His new serial number of A049030 indicated officer status. As a commissioned officer, his life changed drastically that very day, for no longer was he subjected to the ever-present threat of "washing out" and being sent back to the ranks of the enlisted. He quickly perceived a subtle change in the way he was greeted by subordinates and the civilians on the base. Having "won" his wings and a commission, he had proven to the Air Corps that he had the ability to fly their most complicated and expensive airplanes. He also got a much appreciated raise in pay to $150.00 per month, his first "Instrument Card" certifying that he was capable of flying on instruments and a one-time uniform allowance of $200.00! Only then did he get the unwelcome news that his entire class was needed as replacement bomber pilots and so he received his orders to report to B-17 transition training at Roswell AAF Roswell, New Mexico.

WORLD WAR II PILOT"S WINGS

Chapter 2

The Boeing B-17

After about 25 minutes of struggling to stay in the air with only two good engines on the left side, Cornell observed that the number two engine cylinder head temperature gauge had began to climb into the red zone. He now had no choice but to throttle back on that engine and the rate of climb/descent instrument showed the loss of power by increasing the rate of altitude loss. It was only minutes later that the number one engine joined the number two engine in showing signs of overheating. Cornell eased the throttle back on the number one engine. The plane continued to lose precious altitude.

Cornell reconsidered his attempt to reach the coast. All the pilots were aware that the coastline of France, Holland and Belgium was heavily fortified by German anti-aircraft artillery and that the gunners had lots of practice as the 8th Air Force flew over almost daily. Lots of altitude helped somewhat but Cornell's plane was rapidly losing that. Trying to cross the coast at this low altitude would be a sure recipe for disaster.

Plus, the B-17 was not designed as a seaworthy craft and would normally sink a few minutes subsequent to ditching in the water. With bomb bay doors damaged and possibly dangling open, and a large hole in the number three gas tank, the normal few minutes of buoyancy could be restricted to less than a minute. The open bomb bay doors themselves had been known to create enough drag in the water to tear the fuselage in half during a water landing. Also, the North Sea this time of year had a temperature of just above freezing at best, and without question their rubber dinghies, which were located just above the bomb bay, would be tattered and useless.

Then came the clincher. Sergeant Cornelius, the right waist gunner, reported over the intercom that flames—Cornell did not allow his crew to use the word "fire" on the intercom, since this was too alarming—coming from the number two engine near the gas tank. Sgt. Cornelius added that the smoke pouring out was mostly black, which indicated that the fire was being fed by gasoline. The crew listening on the intercom all knew that oil fires, on the other hand, produced mostly white smoke.

Not only had Cornell run out of options, he was quickly running out of time. He continually scanned the distant horizon for some glimpse of the channel, but nothing appeared. This was a hellova time to be missing a navigator. He had no clear idea exactly how far he was from the coast, and it now appeared he could not delay any longer or the B-17 could spin out of control, or worse, explode in mid-air. His thoughts were concentrated on ways to give his crew at least a fighting chance of survival. The crew needed a few desperate seconds of straight and level flying to make their way to the exits and don their parachutes. With tears of helpless anger pooling inside his oxygen mask, Cornell reluctantly ordered his crew to bail out of the crippled B-17. The crewmembers, already standing on ready, were near the exits so they began to jump. Cornell made sure the autopilot was engaged and then unhooked his seatbelt, rose and checked his parachute straps and quickly climbed back into the bomb bay compartment and jumped through the open doors.

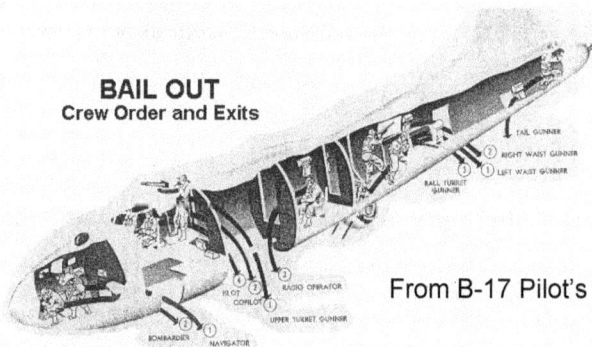

BAIL OUT
Crew Order and Exits

TAIL GUNNER
RIGHT WAIST GUNNER
LEFT WAIST GUNNER
BALL TURRET GUNNER
RADIO OPERATOR
PILOT
COPILOT
UPPER TURRET GUNNER
BOMBARDIER
NAVIGATOR

From B-17 Pilot's Manual

*   *   *   *

In the summer of 1943 when Cornell's class was graduating and receiving their pilot's wings, the most immediate need of the Air Corps at that time was for more heavy bomber pilots and crews to replace the enormous losses of the bombing campaign in Europe. Ergo, Cornell and most of his class was slated to transition into heavy bombers. This entailed yet another transfer by train ride to Roswell Air Base in Roswell, New Mexico. In his short seven months since transferring to the Air Corps, Cornell had trained at four different locations. Similar to his previous bases, Roswell was another training base that was rapidly built at the start of the war. Wooden barracks, administrative buildings, and large wooden hangars were situated beside the seven wide runways reinforced for heavy traffic. Nearby, nine auxiliary fields were constructed for emergencies and to handle the large number of bombers in the air at one time. All of these runways were needed to train pilots for the giant bombers that were coming off the assembly lines. The plane that Cornell was to transition into was the largest plane in the Army Air Corps inventory; the legendary four-engined Boeing B-17.

The Boeing Company, designer of the B-17, got an early start in building giant planes. In 1930 when most airplanes being built were covered in fabric, Boeing developed an all-metal—except for the control surfaces—single-winged plane to compete for the Airmail contracts. They called their creation the "Monomail."

Aviation historians have referred to the plane as the "first modern air transport." The plane was constructed of a smooth stressed aluminum skin and featured retractable landing gear that folded up into the wings. The wings were a new design that incorporated a bridge-like truss inside the wings, thus eliminating external drag-producing wires. The Boeing Company then used the construction techniques they developed in the building of the Monomail to produce a new commercial ten-passenger design, the Boeing 247. The Model 247 incorporated all the advances the Boeing Company had developed; the all-metal construction, retractable landing gear, and internally-braced wings of the Monomail. For designing and building the Model 247, in 1934 the Boeing Company was awarded the Guggenheim Medal, the nation's highest aviation honor, for "successful pioneering and achievement in aircraft manufacture and air transportation."

In 1934 when the Army Air Corps sent out bid requests for a "multiengined" aircraft that could carry 2,000 pounds of bombs over a distance of two thousand miles, the Boeing Company engineers and designers had accumulated the ideal background to compete for the contract. The bid proposal, which promised an order for 220 planes to the winner, was also sent to two other companies with a history in building large multi-engined aircraft, Douglas Aircraft and the Glenn L. Martin Company. When the engineering specifications arrived, the same team that had built the Model 247 was ready to build upon what they had learned to design a new plane, which was given the company designation Model number 299.

The Boeing Model 299 was huge—at the time the largest land plane ever constructed in the United States. The wingspan was over a hundred and three feet and the streamlined aluminum fuselage stretched nearly sixty-three feet from nose to tail. Four huge Pratt & Whitney engines covered with smooth cowlings extended from the wings. Five gun emplacements could be seen emerging from the nose, top, both sides and bottom of the fuselage. The tail stood so tall that interlocks had to be placed on the tall rudder and wide elevators to prevent wind damage when the airplane was parked. According to local legend, when the plane first rolled out of the hangar a visiting newspaper reporter exclaimed, "Why it's a flying fortress!" Regardless, as events would prove or disprove, the name stuck.

Boeing had gambled on designing an airplane with four engines, whereas Douglas Aircraft and the Martin Company chose the more conservative two-engine route. Some skeptics viewed Boeing's choice as being "more complicated that a pilot could handle." Boeing's decision to stake their company on the four-engine route seemed at first to be a wise choice, for in its initial trials the new plane exceeded every expectation. When the new plane was flown from Seattle to Wright Field in Dayton, Ohio in August of 1935, the Model 299 broke all existing records for speed in traveling the 2000 miles non-stop. Officials from Boeing were at Wright Field to welcome the crew who arrived so early the Army Inspectors were not even expecting them yet.

But the B-17 came very close to not becoming a part of America's arsenal of war. For the final evaluation flights of the plane at Wright Field, the Army selected Maj. Ployer P. Hill to test its flying qualities. With another experienced Army pilot in the co-pilot's seat and Boeing Test Pilot Leslie Tower standing behind them, the plane taxied out for its first take-off under the control of Army pilots. At the end of the runway, the plane rose briefly and then rolled, plunged to the ground and burst into flames. Major Hill died and Tower succumbed to burns later in the week.

A full investigation was launched and revealed no fault in the design of the plane. The reason for the crash was traced to the failure of the pilots to remove the parking interlocks on the rudder and elevator controls before they took off. Boeing Test Pilot Tower tried to release the interlocks from where he was standing, but was unable to do so before the plane crashed. Although the crash investigation cleared the airplane design, the crash furnished more ammunition to the critics of the concept of strategic bombing and an expensive fleet of heavy bombers. The non-flying military brass was having trouble absorbing the concept of four giant engines under the control of one crew. The Army immediately reduced the number of planes ordered from the promised 220 to just 13, and gave the rest of the order to the Martin Aircraft Company.

APPROVED B-17 F and G CHECKLIST
REVISED 3-14-1944

BEFORE STARTING
1. Pilot's Preflight-COMPLETE
2. Form 1 A-CHECKED
3. Controls and Seats-CHECKED
4. Fuel Transfer Valves & Switch-OFF
5. Intercoolers-Cold
6. Gyros-UNCAGED
7. Fuel Shut-off Switches-OPEN
8. Gear Switch-NEUTRAL
9. Cowl Flaps-Open Right- OPEN LEFT-locked
10. Turbos-OFF
11. Idle cut-off-CHECKED
12. Throttles-CLOSED
13. High RPM-CHECKED
14. Autopilot-OFF
15. De-icers and Anti-icers, Wing and Prop-OFF
16. Cabin Heat-OFF
17. Generators-OFF

STARTING ENGINES
1. Fire Guard and Call Clear-LEFT Right
2. Master Switch-ON
3. Battery switches and inverters-ON & CHECKED
4. Parking Brakes-Hydraulic Check-On & CHECKED
5. Booster Pumps-Pressure-ON & CHECKED
6. Carburetor Filters-Open
7. Fuel Quantity-Gallons per tank
8. Start Engines: both magnetos on after one revolution
9. Flight Indicator & Vacuum Pressures - CHECKED
10. Radio-On
11. Check Instruments-CHECKED
12. Crew Report
13. Radio Call & Altimeter-SET

ENGINE RUN-UP
1. Brakes-locked
2. Trim Tabs-SET
3. Exercise Turbos and Props
4. Check Generators-CHECKED & OFF
5. Run up Engines

BEFORE TAKEOFF
1. Tailwheel-Locked
2. Gyro-Set
3. Generators-ON

AFTER TAKEOFF
1. Wheel-PILOT'S SIGNAL
2. Power Reduction
3. Cowl Flaps
4. Wheel Check-OK right-OK LEFT

BEFORE LANDING
1. Radio Call, Altimeter-SET
2. Crew Position-OK
3. Autopilot-OFF
4. Booster Pumps-On
5. Mixture Controls-AUTO-RICH
6. Intercooler-Set
7. Carburetor Filters-Open
8. Wing De-icers-Off
9. Landing Gear
a. Visual-Down Right-DOWN LEFT
Tailwheel Down, Antenna in, Ball Turret Checked
b. Light-OK
c. Switch Off-Neutral
10. Hydraulic Pressure-OK Valve closed
11. RPM 2100-Set
12. Turbos-Set
13. Flaps 1/3-1/3 Down

Rarely can a date be set with any precision concerning a standard practice in modern aviation, but the date of the tragedy of the evaluation flight of the Boeing XB-17 on 30 October 1935 marked the birth of the standardized pilot's checklist before taking off. Although the B-17 was not "too much for one pilot to handle," the complicated procedures required for take-off demanded a detailed checklist. Every checklist used today, from an airliner's takeoff to the moon landing, is a direct result of that crash of the Boeing Model 299 in flight evaluation testing at Wright Field in 1935.

Cornell's reception upon his arrival at Roswell Air Base was far different from the greetings at his previous bases. When Lt. Shaddix with the silver wings on his left breast arrived at the Main Gate, he was greeted with a snappy salute from the guards at the gate and asked politely if he needed any assistance with his baggage, and directed to the BOQ, or Bachelor Officer's Quarters for housing. Checking into the base he was provided with an escort and a jeep to make the rounds of delivering his medical records to the base hospital, his pay records to base finance, and his bags to the BOQ. Officers learned quickly to guard their medical records which contained the all-important immunization record which provided proof that they indeed taken all their required shots. If that record was somehow lost, the unlucky soldier had to take them all over again, an ordeal that no one wanted to repeat.

When Cornell began his transition to the B-17 one of the first tasks he had to do was to memorize the B-17 checklist. Although the crew always kept a copy of the checklist in the cockpit, the students had to memorize it for testing purposes. Another task he had to accomplish was to memorize the location of every control and instrument in the B-17 cockpit. He was tested on this by being required to touch every control and point to every instrument while blindfolded in the pilot's seat.

A large portion of the transition training was associated with the fact that the heavy bomber's four engines required much more practice in coping with aeronautical interaction of the multiple engines. Cornell and the other student pilots had to practice flying with one engine shut down, then with two engines shut down, and landing with one or more engines out. They also practiced maneuvering the plane with a dead engine and repeated the routines for dealing with mid-air fires and emergency situations. Cornell did not know at that time how much he was going to use all those exercises in combat.

Although Cornell had done some formation flying in advanced pilot training, his instructors stressed that flying a B-17 in combat required even more tight formations, so the students spent hours delicately adjusting the controls on the four engines in order to ease into close formation with other B-17s. And much more practice in instrument flying, although the weather at Roswell was uniformly good. Many cross-country exercises were undertaken to get used to flying in bad weather and in the darkness.

Flying day and night with powerful planes and maneuvering in close formations by low-time student pilots invariably led to accidents. By the time Cornell had transitioned to heavy bombers he had lost several classmates to accidents, and his instructor at B-17 transition school, whom he had admired greatly, was killed in an aircraft accident a few weeks after Cornell graduated. After successfully completing 125 training hours of flying the B-17, he received his orders to transfer to nearby Pyote AAF in Pyote, Texas to receive his new crew and crew training.

BOEING B-17

The B-17 Cornell was transitioning into was designed to be a strategic bomber. Strategic bombing is usually defined as a method of waging all-out war against an enemy by aerial bombing—in the case of WW2 using long-range heavy bombers—its factories, transportation system, and energy production, especially oil refineries.

This would be differentiated from tactical bombing, which is generally considered to be close air support directly in front of the troops. Although some have considered strategic bombing to include destroying the morale of the enemy, in most cases such attempts, such as the attacks on London in 1940, have accomplished just the exact opposite.

The theory of strategic bombing grew out of the lessons learned in World War 1. Virtually every military leader of the warring factions was appalled at the huge losses of life attributed to the static nature of trench warfare. The more innovative of the combat leaders looked for other ways to defeat an enemy in ways than just sending more men to face each other and die in the trenches. A new innovation they considered was the use of bombing from the rapidly developing technology of airplanes. One of the military theorists to expand on the uses of aerial bombing was the Italian Military Officer Giulio Douhet. Born in 1869, Douhet saw the birth of the airplane and was quick to see its possibilities in warfare. He wrote articles about air power and openly criticized the Italian government for the way it was waging war during WW1. For this criticism Douhet was imprisoned for one year. In his prison cell he began working on a treatise on strategic bombing that later became widely read and quoted. However, his ideas on the effectiveness of massive bombing on civilian morale have been largely disproved by events during WW2. Douhet was later cleared and promoted to General.

In a similar manner, the American General Billy Mitchell, born just ten years after Douhet, was an early advocate of air power, especially the use of bombers against battleships.   Like Douhet, Mitchell openly criticized his superiors for their outdated tactics and antagonized virtually the entire U.S. Navy.   In an experiment in 1921 watched by the Navy Brass and high government officials, Mitchell's bombers easily sank a captured German battleship. As a result of the sinking all Navy budgets were revised downward and the Navy blamed Mitchell personally for the loss in funding. Due to his outspoken manner, Mitchell was demoted to Colonel and later court-martialed for insubordination.   He resigned in 1926 and spent his remaining days writing about the uses of air power. Mitchell's views of air power, especially the vulnerability of battleships to aerial bombers, were confirmed by subsequent events.   The North American B-25 Mitchell bomber, introduced in 1941, was named for General Mitchell, the only military aircraft to be named in honor of a specific person.

Friction had always existed between the U.S. Army and the Navy about the most successful tactics for conducting war. Not only did they disagree on tactics; there was constant competition for funding. The Army felt that more money spent on faster and larger bombers that could carry a heavier load of bombs would better protect American interests both abroad and at home. The Navy felt, on the other hand, that more money spent on larger and more powerful battleships would use the natural barriers of the oceans to better protect the homeland. The

Army was convinced that the new bombers could annihilate even the largest battleship, and the Navy was just as convinced that their newest battleships were virtually invincible. The disagreement led to bitter debates between the services and a constant sniping at each other's theories and plans. Each branch of service spent altogether too much time and energy re-fighting their differences in the political arena, courting congressmen and newsmen to their respective sides. Some Air Corps leaders felt they were in a constant battle with two enemies, first the Navy and then the Germans.

The role of strategic bombing and the new B-17 occupied the very heart of the theories of the Air Corps. The top generals felt that the new heavy bomber would at last prove the concept of destroying an enemy's means of production and fighting and thus end the war earlier or possibly without an invasion. The defensive firepower of the B-17 led the Air Force to believe that massed formations of the heavy bomber could fight their way to the center of the homeland of the enemy even in broad daylight and accurately place their bombs right on the target.

On the other hand, the British had found, just like the Germans, that daylight precision bombing was simply too costly in terms of aircraft attrition. The presence of defending aircraft and deadly anti-aircraft fire from the ground was so devastating that the Germans, and then the British, switched to mostly nighttime bombing missions. With the primitive navigation aids available at that time, nighttime raids were only sporadically effective at specific targets. Hence the British began to utilize area bombing in which the general area of larger targets were saturated with bombs. Some of the bombs were bound to fall near the target, but as a byproduct more civilian casualties were also a result.

However, the Americans felt that certain targets, especially submarine pens, the transportation system, and aircraft plants could only be substantially damaged with sustained daylight missions and at the same time avoiding most of the civilian casualties. The B-17 seemed to be exactly the right weapon to accomplish these goals and the Air Force was determined to give the plane a proper test.

Just like the previous bases where Cornell had been assigned, Pyote Army Air Field was newly built with multiple reinforced runways to be able to withstand the weight of heavy bombers. And just like his previous bases, the buildings were all wooden with some wood-framed covered with tarpaper. Because of the many rattlesnakes that were found in the process of rapidly building the base, it became locally known as the "Rattlesnake Bomber Base." In 1943, at the time Cornell was there, the base was home to over 6,000 military personnel, not counting civilians, and the largest bomber installation in the Air Corps.

After getting settled at Pyote AAF, Cornell was assigned a crew and the group began training together. The Air Force had found that the most successful combat B-17 crews needed a period of indoctrination and training together to be able to fulfill the mission, defend the plane against fighter attacks and to accurately bomb their targets. So the Army Air Corps had adopted a policy of assembling the crews as early as possible and allowing them time to mesh together as a team. The crews were assigned exercises and flights to work together and practice the procedures they would need to survive in combat. Many of the exercises included night flights and simulated bombing runs over selected targets or cities. Since each member was a graduate of one the Army's intensive training programs, the individual crewmembers were fresh out of training school and a little bit nervous about tackling their new assignment and a brand new aircraft commander.

Cornell's new job as pilot in command of a B-17 crew entailed a complete change in the way he approached his daily activities. Where before he was only responsible for himself and his plane, now he was charged with the responsibility of the other nine lives of his crew and a very expensive powerful airplane. Their survival daily depended upon his piloting skills and his decisions. He found his previous training did not adequately prepare him for the responsibilities of command, so he drew upon his knowledge of upbringing in a large extended family where everyone looked out for everyone else and the older kids were responsible for the safety of the younger ones. He quickly absorbed the background and personality of each crewmember and although he was the leader, made sure that each member knew he was interested in them and their comfort. He checked to see that their equipment was complete and their lodging and meals were adequate.

The crew quickly picked up on his rock steady personality and appreciated the way he was interested in each one of them and their different jobs on the plane.

Cornell's newly assembled crew was typically an all-American group. With a pilot from Alabama, the copilot, 2nd Lt. George Sullivan, and navigator, 2nd Lt. Harry Tennenbaum, both hailed from New York, while the bombardier, 2nd Lt. Cole Dailey was from Kansas. The enlisted crew consisted of Technical Sgt. Fred Erb, Radio Operator/Gunner, Technical Sgt. James "Jimmy" Lee, Top Turret Gunner/Engineer, Staff Sgt. John Cortelletty, Ball Turret Gunner, Staff Sgt. William "Corny" Cornelius, Right Waist Gunner, Staff Sgt. Kenneth Hale, Left Waist Gunner, and Staff Sgt. Hugh Hamilton, Tail Gunner.

Cornell found his copilot, George Sullivan, or "Sully" as he wished to be called, was a big easygoing redhead who was a natural pilot and smooth flyer. He often talked of growing up in the Finger Lakes region of New York and his wish to get back there after the war. He and Sully worked together easily and soon trusted the other's piloting ability. Up until now, Cornell had always depended upon his own navigational ability so he was naturally curious to see how his new navigator, Harry Tennenbaum, would work out. With the duties of managing multiple engines and equalizing the flow from multiple fuel tanks while trying to fly in close formation with other bombers, Cornell was far too busy to navigate at the same time. He discovered that Tennenbaum was even more accurate than he had been. Time after time Harry nailed their exact location and came to be a steadying influence with his accurate position reports during bad weather or completely black nights. On longer flights, Harry would call out scenic points or direct the crew's attention to dangers or sights they should not miss. Cornell came to rely completely on Tennenbaum's navigational abilities. In another fortunate assignment, Cornell drew Technical Sergeant James H. "Jimmy" Lee as crew chief and engineer. The short and compactly built Lee, who looked like a coiled spring, was a natural mechanic. He pored over the aircraft technical manuals and came to know more about the mechanical details of the B-17 than any other crewmember. Lee also hailed from Alabama much to the delight of Cornell.

The process of crew training went smoothly and the crew rapidly grew to work as a team, so in January 1944 the group received orders to proceed to Grand Island, Nebraska for their next phase. Grand Island Army Airfield had just been converted in April 1943 to a staging area where bomber crews accepted newly-built bombers, checked them out, and proceeded either to the far Pacific or Europe. Soon after their arrival at Grand Island, Cornell and his group were issued one brand new shiny B-17G, the latest version with more armament, better armor protection for crewmembers, and more powerful engines. The plane incorporated all the changes and additions requested by the combat crews who had been using the plane over enemy territory. One frequent request was more firepower in the nose of the plane, since German pilots had lately discovered that the B-17 was vulnerable to head-on attacks. Even crewmembers in the rear of the plane were in danger from cannon shells fired straight through the plexiglass in the plane's nose.

The new plane delighted the crew and they pored over it, inspecting every nook and cranny and running tests on all its equipment. They took it aloft and practiced maneuvers and takeoffs and landings. Crew Chief "Jimmy" Lee virtually slept in the plane as he made sure the aircraft was up to going into battle. After each flight any minor adjustments or "write-ups" from the crew were immediately seen after by the ground mechanics. A simple request for spare parts brought an immediate response and the parts magically appeared. Cornell and Sgt. Lee were both impressed with the cooperation and attention of Grand Island's supporting base personnel.

Next they were scheduled for preparation for the trip abroad. Each crewmember was supplied with a parachute harness, issued a Mae West, side arms, a knife, and a carefully fitted oxygen mask. Their old flight clothes were replaced with new ones with the addition of several jackets. They were asked to update their records, their booster shots, and reminded to make out their last will and testament. Another medical check was accompanied by a mandatory visit to the dentist for any necessary work before they left.

The crew received orders to proceed with their new B-17 from Grand Island, Nebraska to Grenier Army Airbase in Manchester, New Hampshire for deployment to the European combat theater. This was the first indication that they would be involved in the European Theater rather than the Far East. This mission would be a good test of their piloting and navigation skills before tackling the Atlantic Ocean. The first part of the trip went smoothly as they had been practicing cross-country flights and after landing at Manchester, the crew had several days of briefings and preparation for the second leg of their journey to Goose Bay, Labrador. Upon landing at Grenier they were officially transferred from the Training Command to the Transportation Command, which would be issuing their orders and directing their movements until they reached their final assignment base.

Flying into Goose Bay in the middle of the winter would definitely be an interesting experience. Tales of landing on three feet of packed ice at Goose Bay made Cornell pay close attention to all the advice he could find. In recalling that first landing on ice, Cornell stated, "*On the way up I reasoned that I should be careful to line up precisely with the runway on final approach, using the rudder and brakes as judiciously as possible to reduce the possibility of a slide.*" It worked, and he brought his big bird in neatly. The crew's belief in Cornell's piloting skills and his ability to perform under extreme duress was reinforced.

At Goose Bay the crew watched the locals going out on dog sleds to hunt polar bears, but they were more interested in preparing to tackle the 2,200-mile trip over the Atlantic Ocean in the cold month of January. Even though they had been flying together as a crew for two months and the plane appeared to be reliable, the mere thought of crossing the icy North Atlantic made each crewmember acutely aware of the task facing them. Two days later on 11 February 1944, after insuring that every gas tank was filled to the brim and defrosting one frozen oil line, the crew took off across the Atlantic only sixteen years after Lindbergh had made his historic crossing. Since their path took them just south of Greenland, they were able to spot the enormous chunk of ice in the Arctic twilight and also got their first glimpse of the Aurora Borealis. The crew was momentarily startled in the middle of the ocean to experience visible balls of static electricity called Saint Elmo's Fire that swirled around their plane.

But just as they were approaching the coast of Ireland, the plane experienced a partial electrical failure as their radios and all interior lighting went out. As they spotted their final destination at RAF Nutt's Corner Airfield near Belfast, Ireland, Cornell and the entire crew gained an increased appreciation for the abilities of their navigator, Harry Tennenbaum, who had plotted their destination so precisely. The airfield was a major hub for most American planes arriving across the Atlantic and part of the Royal Air Force Coastal Command. Well aware that they were now running low of fuel, Cornell made several low passes over the field and gently sat the B-17 down on Irish soil. Since the electrical failure the intercom had not worked, but Cornell could hear shouts of relief coming through the fuselage as the plane braked to a stop.

RAF Nutt's Corner Airfield was typical of the bases they would encounter across Britain. Built in record time in 1940, the airfield was composed of the standard triangle of reinforced concrete runways and as the soil was primarily peat bogs, concrete surfaced parking areas for the incoming aircraft. One step into the bog and the pilots did not have to be warned to not allow a wheel to drop off the parking surface. They had never before encountered this type of mud, the kind that seemed bottomless and stuck maddeningly to wheels, tires, and boots. This was the crew's first introduction to rows of Nissen huts, in which they would spend many more nights before they left England. As they checked in with base operations they learned for the first time that their beautiful new shiny B-17–the one they had so carefully checked over and the one that carried them safely across the North Atlantic–was slated to be taken from them. The plane was to be flown to a supply depot to replace a battle-damaged one somewhere in England. They were crestfallen to be in England totally dependent upon trains and trucks for their transportation. The needs of the Army Air Corps come first.

Chapter 3

England and the 8th Air Force

Tumbling through the air, Cornell remembered that they had been briefed repeatedly to delay their parachute opening for as long as possible so as to not present a target for sharpshooters on the ground and also to cut down on the amount of time they would be so highly visible in the air. He was able to spot the already opened parachutes of his crewmembers but he managed to fight off the temptation to pull the "D" ring immediately and free fall. Cornell realized that he probably delayed a moment too long when he saw that he could make out the individual windowpanes of a farmhouse below him. Quickly pulling the D ring of his parachute he was dismayed to find that the pilot chute did not pop out as it was supposed to. He began to frantically pull out hands full of canopy and toss it into the onrushing air until the canopy filled with a loud "Pop!" and the shock of deceleration slowed his fall. But just barely in time, for only two or three seconds elapsed until he slammed into the ground hard, severely hyper-extending his right knee. He had landed in a tall wheat field. Luckily the tall crop hid Cornell, as he just lay there stunned for a few moments. He grimaced in pain from a sudden violent headache and realized he had absolutely no hearing. Swallowing deeply, he cleared the pressure in his eardrums and felt the almost explosive release from the pressure differential brought his hearing back again. He wiped the sweat from his forehead and drew back a bloody hand, leading him to think momentarily that his head had somehow been cut when he exited the plane. But a closer examination revealed that the blood came from the older wounds near his wrist, which had clotted in the cold air of high altitude. The violent landing had somehow caused the wounds to bleed again. He remained hidden in the wheat field as he gathered in the parachute so as to be less conspicuous.

One horrible thought came to him. On each mission, the pilot was issued a "flimsy" which listed the radio frequencies and other pertinent information for the current target. This was printed on what the Air Corps termed "rice paper" and the pilot was instructed to eat the paper in case they going down to prevent the enemy from learning useful information. Cornell realized that in the excitement he hadn't eaten the paper as he was instructed. He hoped the paper might be destroyed in the crash. As he lay there in the field he had never felt so alone or forsaken in his life.

The pain in his knee that had been bent backward was so excruciating that Cornell twisted on his lower leg trying to somehow alleviate the pain. It worked as the knee gave a popping sound as it seemed to maybe slide back in place and the pain eased somewhat. Still unable to walk, he peered out of the tall hay stalks and spotted a haystack in the distance and started trying to crawl to it. It was then that he became aware of two ladies working nearby in the field clad in aprons over long dresses pointing in the opposite direction from Cornell and yelling to him, "Allemand, Allemand!" He had no way of knowing that they were shouting, "German, German!" and trying to warn him to stay where he was. By this time he was nearing the haystack and as he was crawling into it he heard the sound of rapid gunfire. He peeked out to see the German soldiers firing at his crew's parachutes still high in the sky. Much later he found out that they had bailed out virtually over a German garrison. This coincidence explained the almost instantaneous appearance of the enemy soldiers.

Cornell remained hidden in the haystack until nightfall and then started crawling toward a drainage ditch that he had spotted. Entering the ditch, he alternately crawled and hobbled through the drain water—to confuse any dogs that might be following—and tried to continue, with occasional catnaps, throughout the night, but he could not have traveled more than two or three miles. His progress was slowed by his badly swollen knee, which was now beginning to stiffen.

*   *   *   *

In February 1944 when Cornell and his crew flew their new B-17 to England to participate in the air war being waged over the skies of Europe, they were unknowingly joining the greatest air armada in history. He and his crew were just one of many replacements required for the heavy losses the 8th Air Force had been sustaining in conducting daylight precision bombing deep into enemy territory. Early in the war Britain had stood alone in the battle against Germany while Roosevelt and Marshall worked to get America trained and equipped for the ensuing world war that was on the horizon. The 8th Air Force in England was at center stage at this point in the European Campaign.

Even before the events of December 7th, 1941, the Air Force had sent members to England to observe the valiant efforts of the British airmen and to study their aircraft and techniques. They were on hand for the Battle of Britain during the summer and fall of 1940 and gained a new respect for the fighting ability of the Brits. At the same time, the American observers were learning about the limitations of the uses of air power. For one thing, the brave British airmen had withstood the assaults of Goering's bombers and managed, just barely, to inflict enough damage to the German Luftwaffe to cause Hitler to reappraise his tactics. The bombers that did manage to get through to their targets were unable to seriously curtail England's manufacturing output. At the same time, efforts by the Germans to demoralize the British by bombing London and other cities had exactly the opposite effect; the cohesiveness of the British was never closer than during and after the bombing raids.

Nevertheless, both American and British Air Force leaders felt that Germany's industrial might could be damaged and even possibly brought to a halt through strategic bombing alone. What they wanted most was for the allies to give their theories a determined try. The Commander-in-Chief of Britain's Bomber Command, Air Marshall Arthur Harris, felt strongly at the beginning of the war that his bombers were the only group in Britain carrying the war directly to the Germans. Harris fought his superiors continually throughout the war to keep his bombers from being "loaned out" to other missions, such as the invasion of North Africa or the invasion of any area other than Germany itself.

At the same time, the American Brigadier General Ira Eaker was sent to England by General "Hap" Arnold specifically to set up the 8th Bomber Command and to "make the necessary preparations to insure competent command and direction of our bomber units in England." Eaker, a fierce proponent of the use of heavy bombers for strategic warfare, felt that if given a fair chance, the use of strategic bombing alone could possibly bring Germany to its knees and thus end the war without a costly invasion of the mainland.

Eaker arrived in England in early 1942 with a small advance party. His group faced the enormous challenge of making all the preparations for hosting the air armada that was being built and trained in America and would shortly be arriving. They needed to build the reinforced runways, maintenance shops, barracks, and arrange storage for all the equipment and supplies that would be needed to support an all-out strategic bombing effort. Although the British were very accommodating, their industrial capacity was already strained to the utmost. After all, they had been at war for three long years, and with the submarine warfare in the Atlantic and Rommel's victories in North Africa, giving aid to the American effort was not their highest priority at the moment.

Eaker quickly became fast friends with Air Commodore Harris, who did everything in his limited power to assist the American newcomers. Harris saw the Americans as valuable allies to his plans for strategic bombing, and although they did not always agree on tactics, the two leaders coordinated their efforts to bring the war to the German homeland. Harris allocated some airfields in East Anglia to the Yanks and then assisted in converting others and adding even more. Whereas in the past the Americans offered vital assistance to a desperate England with the Lend-Lease program, the British now repaid the favor with interest by helping with the acquisition of real estate, heavy equipment, local labor, and even gasoline when required. In total, 124 air bases were built or converted for the Americans, the single largest construction project in the history of Great Britain.

In studying how to house the over 200,000 airmen who would be arriving over the next year, Eaker's men ordered thousands of Quonset huts from the United States. The ubiquitous semicircular hut was an adaptation of the earlier British Nissen Hut. Invented during World War I by Major Peter Nissen of the British Royal Engineers as a better solution to the problem of housing soldiers, the solid structure was much better than temporary tents. The main appeal was the speed in which the huts could be bolted together. During World War II the Nissen Company waived their patent rights so American production began at Quonset Point, Rhode Island. Although the prefabricated huts were also built in other locations, they became known as Quonset Huts in the United States rather than Nissen huts in England. The galvanized corrugated sections were capable of being nested so they took up less space to transport and required no skilled labor to erect on site. They could be placed on concrete, plywood, tongue-and-groove lumber or even on bare ground. They withstood high winds so they were especially valuable in the extreme northern areas. Although some huts, such as those used for infirmaries and offices were insulated, most of the other ones used as barracks were not. A small coal heater placed in the center lessened the damp chill but did not really warm the hut. Virtually all the American airmen living in the British Isles resided in Quonset huts. Over 150,000 of the huts were produced during the war and most were disassembled and sold as surplus property after the war. A few still remain as historic reminders of the many airfields built during World War II.

Another brilliant innovation aided the Americans as they struggled to ship the millions of pounds of clothing, weapons, ammunition, food, tools, and parts needed to the European theatre. This was the introduction and use of the ubiquitous wooden pallet. The increasing use of gasoline-powered forklifts in the late 1930s led to the adoption at the beginning of the war of a standard wooden pallet to speed the loading and unloading of ships and trains. The Navy was quick to adopt this new method of shipping. The powered forklift and use of wooden pallets magically reduced the time and workload of moving supplies. The British in particular were astounded at the speed in which the American Navy could unload supplies on their docks. Later historians of logistics agreed that the widespread use of pallets led to a quantum leap in the Allies' ability to move supplies to distant shores. Today's giant containers on the ships that cross the oceans are the direct descendent of the humble wooden pallet developed by the U.S. Military.

In discussing his relationship with General Eaker, Air Marshall Harris stated: "My attitude to him and his Command . . . is that if we possess anything he wants. . . everything 'up to the half of my kingdom' is his for the asking." Harris did try to convince Eaker to forgo daylight bombing missions—concentrating instead on night missions—until they had gained more experience, but Eaker was determined to try out his theories in daylight precision bombing. The idea of round-the-clock bombing with the British on missions virtually every night and the Americans bombing almost every day did appeal to the Chief Air Marshall.

Using British bases as a beginning, Eaker and his crew began to convert and build air bases in eastern England until they occupied almost 100 bases for the 8th Bomber Command alone. The first combat crews with their new B-17s began arriving in August 1942 after meeting the challenge of navigating across the Atlantic Ocean on their own. Not all the B-17s that attempted the crossing with brand new planes and inexperienced crews made it successfully; some were lost due to weather or running off the runways, but the loss percentage was less than 4%. The new arrivals immediately started practicing close formations and getting up to speed in flying through the changeable English weather. Having mostly trained in the sunny southwestern United States, the American flyers were not really prepared for the almost constant cloudy skies and heavily overcast conditions of the British Isles.

General Eaker explained the mission of the 8th Air Force: "*First [destroy] the factories, sheds, docks, and ports in which the enemy builds his submarines...Next his factories and other key munitions-manufacturing establishments. Third, his lines of communications.*" On August 17, 1942, the 8th flew their first short mission to bomb the railroad marshalling yards at Rouen, France, with British Spitfires escorting the B-17s. The mission was successful and all 12 planes returned safely. The lead pilot for the mission was Capt. Paul Tibbets, who would later become known as "the best pilot in the Air Force" and be chosen to pilot General Eisenhower's plane for several critical trips during the war. After this first mission, General Eaker stated: "*The raid went according to plan and we were satisfied with the day's work. But one swallow doesn't make a summer.*" After 25 more missions, Tibbets' group, the 97th Bomber Group, was then transferred to North Africa, where he flew for Major General Jimmy Doolittle's 12th Air Force. Chief of the Air Corps General

"Hap" Arnold asked Doolittle to recommend an experienced pilot to help work the bugs out of the new B-29 bomber that was having developmental problems. Doolittle recommended Tibbets, who returned to the states and took over the troubled project. This directly led to Tibbets piloting the *"Enola Gay"* on the first atomic bomb mission in 1945.

Eaker's premonition about the success of the daylight bombing campaign was correct. The next several missions were successful with only minor losses, but they were shorter missions with constant fighter support. However, as the missions grew longer and deeper into France, the British fighters were unable to accompany the groups the entire distance so the losses to enemy fighters began to mount. The German fighters were fearlessly attacking the bomber groups, slashing through the formations and trying new tactics almost every mission.

At the same time, the planned invasion of North Africa was taking a higher priority, so incoming aircraft and airmen were diverted to that theatre. Consequently, replacement planes and crews were not available to make up for the losses. In the fall of 1942 the strength of the 8th Air Force in England began to suffer as the mechanics struggled to repair their planes without adequate spare parts. The decision to support the North African campaign was proving costly to the efforts of the 8th Air Force to prove that strategic bombing could alter the course of the war.

Daylight bombing of the German homeland by the 8th Air Force began early in 1943. The first missions were successful but the need for fighter support all the way to the target and back was made clear by the losses sustained. Maj. Curtis LeMay was the commander of the newly created 305th Bomb Group, which had been transferred to England in October 1942. After their earliest missions over Germany, LeMay pored over the photos of the results and was distinctly unhappy about the percentage of bombs that had fallen on the target. As a result of his research, he initiated a new policy of maintaining straight and level flight throughout the bomb run, which angered many of his pilots, because they thought it would be suicidal. But the results showed in the bombing aftermath photos; invariably LeMay's Group plastered the target accurately. As a result, his bombing methods were adopted across the entire 8th Air Force.

In another controversial move, LeMay insisted on tighter formations, which gave increased firepower, but was difficult for the low-time pilots to maintain with the heavy multiengine bombers. Nevertheless, his idea of the "combat box formation" won out and was adopted and followed by the rest of bomber command. For his leadership, LeMay was promoted and sent to lead the 20th Bomber Command in China.

The 8th Air Force Commanders tried out other different tactics to cut their losses. Tighter formations, more gunnery practice, diversionary groups to draw off fighters from the main attacking force and more bombers on the mission were some of the changes adopted. The German defenders also changed tactics. One of their most effective tactics was to direct their interceptors to concentrate on just one group within the Bomber stream. Although the main force could force its way to the target, one unit of the massed formation would suffer devastating losses, in some cases, almost wiping out that group.

This tactic of concentrated attacks on one Bomber group within the vast formation led directly to the legend of the "Bloody 100th." On 17 August 1943 on a mission to Regensburg, the 100th Bomb Group drew the dreaded "Tail-end Charlie" position in the formation and lost 9 planes and a total of 90 men to the altered tactics of the German defenders. On 8 October 1943 on a mission to Bremen the 100th drew the high group formation, another vulnerable spot and lost 7 more planes with a loss of 72 men. Two days later on 10 October on a mission to Munster the Group lost 12 planes with a loss of 121 men. On the Munster mission, only 1 B-17 from the 100th Bomb Group was able to return to their base at Thorpe Abbotts! Over the next two years, the 100th Bomb Group did not fly the most missions, nor did they drop the most bombs or suffer the most casualties, but the early losses of 28 planes in only three missions led to the nickname "Bloody 100th", an appellation that no one wanted.

By 1943, the Air Force brass had realized that the average bomber crew could only complete 8 to 12 missions before being shot down or disabled. For this reason, the commanders decided that any flying crews with the 8th Air Force assigned to the heavy bomber units who completed 25 missions would be rotated back to the states because of the "physical and mental strain on the crew." Although the number was high, having a distinct goal gave hope to the crews that they might actually survive their tour. The first aircrew publicized for reaching the magical 25 missions was the crew of the *Memphis Belle*, although other crews may have been earlier. The publicity came about from the efforts of the Hollywood director William Wyler, who placed cameramen on several of the planes that had high mission numbers. When the *Memphis Belle* achieved 25 missions, they were sent back to the states for a three-month war bond and morale boosting tour. Wyler's documentary film *The Memphis Belle,* which contained actual combat footage, made the plane and the crew widely known.

In 1949, the movie *"Twelve O'clock High"* starring Gregory Peck was a thinly disguised version of those tragic days. The plane featured in most of the scenes, *"The Piccadilly Lilly"* was the name of one of the 100th Bomb Group planes lost on the 8 October mission to Bremen. The screenwriter of the movie and co-author of the book, Colonel Bernie Lay, Jr. often visited the 100th and flew the Regensburg shuttle mission with them in *The Piccadilly Lily.* Although parts of the film were shot in England, the takeoffs and landings were taken at a closed World War II airbase in South Alabama. The B-17 crash landing sequence by famed movie stuntman Paul Mantz was also filmed there. The film garnered four Academy Award nominations and won two; Best Supporting Actor and best Sound Recording. In 1998, the Library of Congress placed the film on the National Film Registry for being being "culturally, historically, or aesthetically significant."

General Eaker observed the toughness of the B-17 and how it could withstand numerous hits and still remain flying and bring its crew home. After the war he offered an assessment of the the plane: "The B-17, I think, was the best combat airplane ever built. The B-17 was a bit more rugged than the B-24. It could ditch better because of the low wing, and it could sustain more battle damage. You wouldn't believe they could stay in the air." General Curtis LeMay, later Chief of Staff of the Air Force agreed: "...the Air Force kind of grew up with the B-17. It was as tough an airplane as was ever built. It was a good honest plane to fly-a pilot's airplane. It did everything we asked it to do, and did it well."

After landing at RAF Nutt's Corner in Ireland and having their beautiful new B-17 taken from them, Cornell and his crew made their way across the British Isles, all by means other than air, including truck, train, and boat. After resting from their flight, the crew took a train and then a ferry across the Irish Sea to Liverpool, England where they attended an orientation school for about three weeks. While at Liverpool the crew got its first taste of the air war when Liverpool suffered one of its frequent night bombing attacks by the Germans. The crew was supposed to retire to a underground concrete bomb shelter but they sat on top of the shelter to be able to view the aerial show of searchlights, tracers, bombs going off, and aircraft droning and crashing.

At the completion of the orientation school, the newly arrived crews checked by the "Head Shed", or headquarters, to check on which outfit they were headed for. When Cornell and Sully appeared at the office looking for some word about their next assignments, the Officer-in-Charge silently handed them their orders and stood by looking down as they read the long list of instructions. Their new assignment was to the 100th Bomb Group of the

8th Air Force, located at Thorpe Abbotts Airfield about 110 miles northeast of London. Only later when Cornell learned of the story of the "Bloody Hundredth" did he understand the strange behavior of the officer.

From Liverpool, Cornell and his crew traveled by train past small thatched cottages, quaint old country inns, ancient churches, and mostly pastures full of cattle and sheep to a small village named Diss, England where on 11 March 1944 they were deposited at the train station to await transportation. They were met by a personnel carrier, a truck with a canvas covered bed that contained two benches along the sides, from the air base. As they traveled in the back of the truck they noticed the narrow roads and the fact that their driver drove on the wrong side of the road.

Thorpe-Abbotts in East Anglia

Thorpe-Abbotts airfield was originally built in 1942 and 1943 as a field for the RAF, but was handed over to the 8th Air Force in 1943, who promptly enlarged it during the rapid buildup of the Air Force in England. Occupying about 500 acres, the air base had three runways with the main one being 6,300 feet long and over three miles of perimeter track, all reinforced concrete, with about 300 buildings, shops, Nissen huts, and hangars. It was very much like a small city, with a Post Office, Military Police, a hospital, a Fire Department, a church, recreational facilities, and of course a Red Cross unit. In support of the bombing missions the base contained units responsible for ordinance, armament, communications, transportation, photography, and a petroleum section for the hundreds of thousands of gallons of aviation fuel required weekly.

Photo courtesy Rik Verhelle

Cornell and his crew. He is kneeling on the left

The base occupied parts of what used to be two very large farms and sheep still grazed in the fields and farmers tilled the soil with horses just outside the runways. Two of the older thatch-roofed homes still remained on the base. Rows of long low Nissen huts lined the access roads on the base, interspersed by an occasional barn. The only identification of the location of their assigned Squadron headquarters, the 349th, was that the Nissen hut had a bulletin board on the front wall. They were introduced to their new Squadron Commander, Captain Sumner Reeder, in a very somber greeting.

Three months earlier, Reeder, then a Lieutenant, was piloting a B-17 on a mission to Stuttgart when four fighters attacked his plane from a head-on position while he was on his final bomb run. The fighters, armed with 20 mm. cannons, shot through the cockpit of Reeder's plane, killing his co-pilot and seriously wounding the bombardier and navigator. The shell that killed the copilot also wounded Reeder and knocked out the oxygen system and punctured one wing tank. Reeder put the B-17 into a dive to a lower cloudbank and successfully eluded the fighters in a deadly game of hide-and-seek as he went from cloud to cloud, always going lower and lower because the crew had no oxygen other than the portable bottles. With the help of the wounded navigator, who had lost an eye, the dying copilot was removed from the shattered cockpit and the navigator took his place. The wounded Reeder managed to pilot the plane back to England and set the B-17 down with no brakes on the first RAF fighter base he could find. Reeder was awarded the Distinguished Service Cross for his actions.

Cornell and his crew were quickly educated in the lore and background of the "Bloody Hundredth." The officers were assigned to bunk in one Nissen hut while the enlisted men were assigned to another. Several days passed before Cornell learned that all 16 of the previous occupants of the hut had failed to return from their last mission, hence the availability of plenty of beds. In Cornell's hut he made friends with the officers from three other aircrews who had all just arrived days before Cornell. The first, Frank Harte, was shot down by a gaggle of FW-190s on a mission to Hamm while Cornell watched helplessly from his cockpit in the tight formations. Cornell learned later that Lt. Harte, along with his navigator, were bludgeoned to death after they parachuted to the earth. Cornell and his crew went next. The other two crews in Cornell's hut lasted a few more days. The next, 1st Lt. Ralph Horne successfully ditched in the cold Baltic after being shot up in a long mission to Berlin on May 5th. The crew was able to escape the sinking B-17 and make it to shore but was captured in Denmark and spent the rest of the war in various German POW camps. Cornell managed to meet Horne after the war and they joked about trying to escape the German navy. The last pilot in Cornell's original hut group was 2nd Lt. Lawrence "Larry" Townsend, whose B-17 was shot down by antiaircraft fire while providing ground support for the rapidly advancing allied troops near St. Lo, France in July 1944. Townsend and his crew were able to bail out of their crippled plane and were captured by the Germany Army and spent the rest of the war in a POW camp.

Cornell and his crew quickly acclimated to their new quarters, but they had as yet not been assigned an airplane. There were many differences in their new base from the Air Corps bases they had been stationed in the sunny southwestern United States. The weather was markedly different, for the airfield seemed to be foggy or overcast half of the time. The entire air base, including the barracks, officer's club and even the latrine, was wired for public address speakers, which the British called the "Tannoy," from the name of the speaker manufacturer. The PA system was in constant use as it broadcast all pertinent meetings, warnings, and even sometimes called someone by name to an important appointment. Another change that was immediately apparent to Cornell and his crew was the absence of airmen constantly saluting their senior officers. On their stateside training bases, saluting was a constant reminder of discipline, but life in a war zone was markedly different. Personnel in flying clothes, both Officer and Enlisted, seemed to ignore the rules of saluting, and mechanics hurrying to the bombers with both hands full of tools or parts just forgot about saluting. Cornell and his men had of course already dropped the habit of saluting each other as they trained together. About the only time a salute was deemed necessary on their new base was when an airman was formally reporting to a superior officer.

Situated near their Nissen hut barracks were the latrines, which consisted of a ditch lined with two rows of dirt located between two concrete walls. At one end of the latrine was a tall pole that held two colored light bulbs. The men learned that when the green light was lit, they

were "stood down" or free to go about as they chose. A
lighted red bulb meant that the crew was on alert for a
mission so the club was closed and the men were not
allowed to leave the base proper. Since the base was
rather spread out and getting about took some time, most
of the men quickly purchased or traded for an English
bicycle, usually from anther service member and brushed
up on their riding skills. Because none of the bicycles
were equipped with the American type coaster or
"backpedal" brakes, but rather the English type rim
brakes that were operated by hand levers, the largest
source of injuries to newcomers was from learning to ride
the different type of bike. Cornell purchased his from
another pilot who was transferring back to the states

A few days after Cornell and his crew arrived at
Thorpe-Abbots, the new commander of the 8th Air Force,
General Jimmy Doolittle, arrived in a specially modified P-
38. Doolittle was a hero of Cornell's:

*"Since early childhood I had held Jimmy Doolittle as
an idol as did many other kids of the time. He participated
in air races around pylons in which those fast (for the time)
aircraft were operated perilously close to the ground and
each other. He also was the first man to make a completely
blind flight from beginning of takeoff to end of landing roll.
He simply was a superb, skillful pilot."*

Later Doolittle assembled the flying crews in the
largest building for a short address in which he stated
how he regretted the losses that the unit had been
sustaining. He explained that for the immediate future
the 100th Bomb Group would be centered within the
flying formations to be better protected by the massing of

guns. Cornell noted that Doolittle wore only one ribbon under his pilot's wings, the ribbon that signified the holder of the Congressional Medal of Honor. Doolittle's easygoing manner and sense of humor won over Cornell and all the crewmembers.

Although Doolittle's fame was overshadowed by his role in leading the famous raid on Tokyo in 1942, he would have otherwise easily gone down in the history of aviation for his many earlier accomplishments. As an early aviator in the birth of a new technology, Doolittle was constantly in the forefront of efforts to improve aeronautical sciences and promote the use of airplanes in commerce and the military.

Born in California in 1896, James Harold "Jimmy" Doolittle attended Los Angeles City College and studied at the University of California at Berkeley. In 1917 he enlisted in the Signal Corps and as a flying cadet was commissioned a Lieutenant in 1918. During WW 1, Doolittle was a Flight and Gunnery Instructor. Discovering that he absolutely loved flying and the life of an Army pilot, Doolittle remained in the Army to be involved in aviation. In those early days of aviation, Army pilots were often allowed to enter competitions and to perform exhibitions and demonstrations. Commanders soon realized that Washington was interested in record-setting and other newsworthy projects that would create a favorable image of the Army Air Service. Doolittle's can-do attitude fit right in with the Army's post-war approach to aviation. While stationed at Rockwell Field, San Diego, California, the eager young Doolittle caught the attention of the base commander, Col. Henry H. "Hap" Arnold.

Arnold, who advanced in rank to become the Chief of Staff for the Army Air Corps, would later prove to be instrumental in Doolittle's military career. With Arnold's permission, Doolittle attempted and set many long-distance and speed records to prove what airplanes could do and to publicize Army aviation.

In 1920 Doolittle graduated from the Army's Air Service and Mechanical School at Kelly Field in Texas, which was the start of his long career in investigating and understanding the physics of flying. Meanwhile, he continued to set long-distance records for the Army, including one solo coast-to-coast trip from Florida to California for which he was awarded the Distinguished Flying Cross. But when Doolittle was accepted to attend the Air Service Engineering School at McCook Field in Dayton, Ohio in 1922, he found his true calling. The school was the Air Service's postwar aviation research center, and was a one year course that covered mechanics, armament, materials, electricity, power plants, and theoretical aeronautics. A compelling case could be made that in this assignment, Doolittle effectively became the nation's first test pilot. His precise engineering approach to flying an unfamiliar airplane meshed perfectly with McCook's mission to understanding the flying qualities of all new airplanes. While at the Engineering School, Doolittle flew virtually every type of airplane available to the Army at that time. He investigated and developed aids to flying in bad weather, the use of parachutes—which saved his life several times—and aircraft stability and control.

After Doolittle finished the school, friends persuaded him to apply for one of the six positions offered by the Army to attend the Massachusetts Institute of Technology for a master's degree in Aeronautical engineering. He was accepted so in 1923 he was given two years to complete his degree. Doolittle credited his wife, Josephine, for most of his academic success for she typed his class notes daily, went over them with him and helped prepare him for his examinations. He still flew as much as possible and used the Army's planes to research his master's thesis, which was an investigation into the flying stresses on a pilot and a plane's structure using a recording accelerometer. His research was some of the first precision calibrations performed on actual airplanes under flying conditions. Doolittle later received a second Distinguished Flying Cross for these contributions.

Since Doolittle had finished his master's degree in one year, he decided to apply for permission to use the second year to work toward a doctorate. His application was approved so he completed the required course work in the following year and was subsequently transferred back to McCook Field where he continued his research and worked on his dissertation, "*The Effect of Wind Velocity Gradient on Airplane Performance.*" When the faculty of MIT accepted it in 1925, Doolittle was awarded the Doctor of Science degree in Aeronautical Sciences, one of the earliest such degrees on the United States.

Back at McCook, Doolittle was made chief of the Flight Test Division with the chance to combine both of his passions, flying and engineering. While in this position, Doolittle received another lucky opportunity; he was contacted by Harry F. Guggenheim, son of the philanthropist who had established a multi-million dollar organization entitled the "Guggenheim Fund for the Promotion of Aeronautics." The Guggenheims had come to realize that the real barrier to continued progress in aviation was the problem of flying in fog, night, or bad weather. With the Army's blessing, in 1928 Doolittle was granted a year of "detached service" to work with the foundation to develop blind flying instruments and techniques.

Doolittle worked with Elmer Sperry, Jr. to develop and test the first artificial horizon and directional gyroscope. He also got the opportunity to work with Paul Kollsman to develop and test a new improved altimeter that was much more accurate. Both instruments later became standard equipment for instrument flying. He coordinated with U.S. Bureau of Standards to develop electrical equipment both on the end of airport runways and airborne to guide the plane during landing. Using these and other instruments, he was the first pilot in the world to take off and land an airplane completely "blind" without referring to the outside of the cockpit. Years later, Doolittle felt that these contributions to aviation during this year of research and development were the most significant of his entire career.

However, in 1930 Doolittle received an offer to head the aviation department of Shell Oil that paid three times his Army salary. Resigning his Army commission was probably the hardest decision that Doolittle had to make, but his family obligations to his wife and two sons took precedent. While with Shell, Doolittle led the effort to develop higher octane gasoline for commercial and military aviation uses. Since Shell Oil was interested in publicity for its aviation fuels, they permitted Doolittle to enter a few air races. In the 1931 Bendix Air Race, he established a new coast-to-coast record of 11 hours and 11 minutes, the first time anyone had flown this distance in less than 12 hours. But it was his victories as the pilot of the infamous Gee-Bee Air Racer that gave Doolittle his greatest public acclaim. The Gee-Bee, designed by the Granville Brothers, had the promise of being the fastest plane on earth, but it also had the reputation of killing its pilots. Virtually a tiny set of wings attached to a huge radial engine, the plane required constant correction to remain level and was very tricky to take off or land. In qualifying for the 1932 Thompson Air Races, Doolittle set a new world speed record of 309.040 miles per hour, which made him officially the fastest traveling human on earth. The Gee-Bee Racer was faster than all the military aircraft at that time. He also won the race, competing against the top racers in the nation. Shortly afterward, Doolittle announced that he was retiring from air racing, citing his advanced age of 34 and the desire to get back to engineering and his job with Shell Oil.

In June 1940, Doolittle received a letter from Gen. Ira Eaker, asking if he would consider coming back on active duty to help the Air Corps solve reliability problems with their new aircraft engines. The challenge appealed to Doolittle and his patriotism would allow no other course, so with the blessing of Shell Oil, he went directly to the Allison Engine plant in Indianapolis to start work. But because he had missed flying in combat in World War I, Doolittle kept up a campaign for a flying assignment.

Not long after the events at Pearl Harbor, Air Corps Chief "Hap" Arnold called Doolittle into his office and asked "Jim, what airplane do we have that can take off in 500 feet, carry a 2,000-pound bomb load, and fly 2,000 miles with a full crew?" Dolittle, with his background in aeronautical engineering, answered, "General, give me a little time and I'll give you the answer." Doolittle not only recommended the Mitchell B-25; he also campaigned to lead the raid on Tokyo. A few days later Gen. Arnold responded, "Okay, it's your baby. You'll have first priority on anything you need to get the job done. Get in touch with me directly if anyone gets in your way."

Doolittle chose the tactics and led the crew selection, the training, and the logistics involved in supporting the mission. Keeping the Tokyo mission a secret caused many difficulties but on 18 April 1942 Lt. Col. Doolittle led the first air raid on the capitol of Japan. The raid proved the vulnerability of the Japanese to air attack and worked wonders for morale at home. Although Doolittle feared he would be court-martialed because all the planes were lost, he was promoted two grades to Brigadier General and awarded the Medal of Honor.

Doolittle's next combat command was commander of the Twelfth Air Force operating in North Africa, where he was promoted to Major General in 1942. Still he continued to fly on missions to learn more about enemy tactics and anti-aircraft weaponry. When he heard about Doolittle's occasional flying on missions, his boss Eisenhower reprimanded him privately, but he still recommended Doolittle's promotion. In January 1944, just before the time Cornell and his crew were arriving in England, Doolittle was given command of the 8th Air Force, at that time the largest command in the Air Corps, and promoted to Lieutenant General, the highest ranking reserve officer in the Air Corps

When Doolittle landed in England he lost no time in assuming complete command of the 8th Air Force. He made the rounds of the units under his command, personally meeting the airmen and making changes in defensive tactics. In studying the mission losses, Doolittle ordered his fighter planes to accompany the bombers all the way to the target and back. This was only possible because of the increased number of long-range fighter planes now available. The presence of defensive fighter planes made a difference in the losses from air attacks, but the losses from anti-aircraft artillery continued as before.

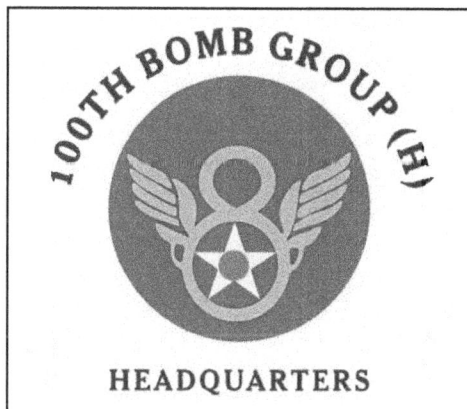

100TH BOMB GROUP (H)

HEADQUARTERS

Chapter 4

Missing In Action

Cornell was cold, wet, exhausted, and hungry when daylight finally crept in where he lay beside the small water-filled ditch that he had been following. His knee was even more painful after the night of trying to escape. The day previous to his being shot down he and his crew had gotten up at 2:30, taken off just before sunrise, completed a short mission, returned to England, refueled, reloaded with bombs, and headed out for a second mission. It had been a very long stressful day and night. He rummaged through the survival kit that the crews had been issued. It contained a small compass, some matches in a waterproof container, a map of France and the low countries, two thousand in French francs, and some other odds and ends, including a shot of morphine, but Cornell never considered using it because he wanted to keep his head clear. Dragging his injured leg, he rustled up some fallen branches beside the ditch and made a small fire to warm himself. He resigned himself to the thought of being captured.

Then from the corner of his eye he saw two young fellows, both just barely teenagers, cautiously approaching. They were both clad in short pants with socks up to their calves and appeared very trim and polite. They continued to scan up and down the creek bank as they walked beside their bicycles and edged closer. In very broken English the older of the two haltingly asked if they could help. Cornell tried to rise and they could see that he was in pain and only able to move with difficulty. He sank back to the ground. They looked around furtively and hurriedly put out the fire and with gestures and more broken English indicated they would be back shortly. Cornell had no choice but to lie there and wait for their return. Only minutes later they returned with an extra bicycle.

Helping Cornell to straddle the bicycle, they pushed him out to the highway that he had been avoiding and quickly across to a canal and into a wooded lane that ran parallel to but hidden from the road by a line of trees. Dragging one leg and pushing with the other, Cornell used the bicycle as a crutch with wheels to follow his new friends to a small town that he would later learn to be Izegem, Belgium.

They passed several houses before getting off their bikes at a neatly trimmed cottage of white-washed brick with a red tile roof. It had deeply set windows indicating that the walls were very thick. The boys wasted no time easing Cornell off his bicycle and into the house. Just inside the door Cornell spied an older couple, who, seeing that he was grimacing in pain, indicated for the lads to help Cornell to a chair near a table. The stocky gray-haired woman with her braided hair wrapped around her head reminded Cornell of his aunt Docia. Their smiles made him feel less fearful. The older man, whose gray mustache had almost turned white, spoke a few words to the boys and then, peering both ways through the open door, motioned for them to go and quickly closed the door behind them. The older woman approached Cornell with a wet cloth and a glass of water, never ceasing her constant flow of unintelligible words with the old man. Cornell had no idea what they were discussing, but it quickly became clear as they bustled about cleaning him up that they meant him no harm but were trying to help. He was about to the limit of his endurance and this must have been evident to the older couple. The man helped Cornell move to a bedroom in the rear of the cottage where he motioned for him to try the bed. Gingerly lowering himself, Cornell stretched out and found his feet hanging completely off the end of the bed. No matter. In minutes he was sound asleep and must have slept for twelve hours or more.

*   *   *   *

The 100th Bomb Group, like most other Groups in the 8th Air Force, made a practice of scheduling all new replacement pilots to fly their first mission as a copilot with a veteran aircrew. So while his crew anxiously waited, Cornell drew his first mission on 16 March 1944 to fly as copilot on a mission to bomb an airport near Munich. They would be accompanied by P-51s fitted with the new long-range disposable fuel tanks. Cornell had already become acquainted with the pilot of the plane he was assigned to, 1st. Lt. Floyd "Bucky" Mason who was a fellow Alabamian. He felt privileged to fly alongside the veteran Mason who had acquired a reputation as being a fine pilot under stress.

Cornell was awakened by the squadron orderly about 2:30 in the morning. By this time he had the routine down pat. First he climbed into his long knitted underwear, or "long johns," blue flannel underwear wired for connection to the plane's electrical heating system, wool pants and shirt and low-cut brown military oxford shoes. Over this went his flying coveralls, fleece-lined boots, leather fleece-lined flying jacket, fleece-lined pants, and his cap. Normally the crew kept their gloves and helmets in the plane, so Cornell had to bring along his own. The helmet was donned as the B-17 entered the area of intense flak during the bomb run. Outside, a personnel carrier was slowly cruising in front of the Nissen huts, picking up crews to transport them to Group Operations for the briefing. The building was one of the largest on the base, able to hold some 250 men who were filing in as Cornell and the rest of Mason's crew entered. They were mostly quiet, but the Red Cross workers were already in place offering coffee and doughnuts to the men. Cornell followed Mason as he went down to the front rows, close to the raised stage with two easels in front of a huge map covered with a black curtain on a wire. Cornell spotted his Squadron Commander, Capt. Reeder, who nodded to the crew. The place was mostly full of lieutenants and captains when a loud command "At-ten-HUT" brought the men to their feet. Down the center aisle marched the Group Commander, Col. Neil Harding, followed by the weather officer and several others.

"Seats, men," he said as he motioned to the Briefing officer standing by the side of the stage. The Briefing officer pulled back the curtain dramatically and a slight rustle swept through the audience as they saw a red ribbon stretched from Thorpe Abbotts to a rendezvous point just before they would cross the English Channel to deep within Germany to Gablingen Air Field near Augsberg and Munich. The Briefing officer went over the routes, the timing, the altitude, and the radio codes. The Group Navigator discussed the checkpoints, and asked if there are any questions. There were not too many questions. Then the men loaded back up in the personnel carriers to the Flying Officer's Mess. The smell entering the mess was mouth watering, a mixture of bacon, pancakes, syrup, and coffee. The breakfast was excellent, but Cornell took only a sip of the coffee for he knew the length of the cumbersome passage back to the relief tube in the bomb bay area.

Then back on the trucks for the ride out past the control tower to the concrete hard stand where Mason's plane was located. Although it was slowly become lighter, daybreak had still not arrived to burn away the morning mist when he jumped down from the truck. He could just make out the other planes nearby. Cornell never got used to the way the chilly English mornings seemed to chill his bones. The airfield was coming alive as the planes were being prepared for battle. Cornell spotted Mason's crew already at the plane, oiling their machine guns but not saying much. They glanced at the strange copilot, but no one offered to come over and greet the newcomer. The hatch under the cockpit was open, so Cornell tossed his gear and parachute up through the hatch, then pulled his body up into the plane.

Just getting off safely in the chilly morning with fuel tanks filled to the brim and a full bomb load was a challenge; then Mason had to delicately maneuver the plane into their assigned spot within the mass of bombers arriving from other bases to assemble into one giant formation. Fitting this many giant bombers into the combat box formation, sometimes in cloudy weather, often led to accidents. During the period 1943 until 1945, the 100th Bomb Group lost 177 aircraft missing in action plus 52 lost due to operational accidents. Thus almost one-third of all losses were from accidents, not enemy action.

Cornell's first mission was perhaps an accurate indicator of the hazards of the ones to follow for they were attacked at times throughout the entire mission by German ME-109s, even though they had the benefit of being escorted by six P-51s. Cornell witnessed a P-51 diving through the middle of his formation, barely squeezing in between his plane and the one on their wing. A split second later, Cornell caught sight of the reason for the P-51's suicidal dive; on his tail was a ME-109 with all guns blasting, who in turn was followed closely by another P-51 firing at the German plane. The second P-51 must have scored because Cornell then observed the canopy fly off the ME-109.

The skies were overcast most of the way to the target and the crew fretted that they would not be able make an accurate bomb drop, but most of the clouds dissipated just before they arrived at the Air Field. Cornell could clearly see smoke arising from the previous bombs dropped by the planes ahead. At the signal "Bombs away!" the plane leaped upward as the heavy bomb load fell. The flak over the target was not as heavy as it would become much later. The flak lessened as they left the built-up industrial area, but the German planes continued to make strafing runs on their formation.

Probably because of their position deep within the massed group, the 100th did not lose any planes, but during the entire mission 18 B-17s were lost with a loss of 171 crewmembers and 10 more wounded in the planes that were able to make it back. Mason's crew was credited with shooting down one German plane. After each combat mission all members of the combat crews were given one ounce of Scotch whiskey to "relax the tension." But after tasting the first one, thereafter Cornell gave his to whoever wanted another because he discovered he really disliked the taste and the throat scorch that accompanied the stiff drink. After they landed, Cornell's crew got him aside and pummeled him with questions about the mission, the amount of flak, the enemy fighters, and how close the formation was retained. The gunners especially wanted to know his perception of the speed of the interception of the enemy planes.

Finally, their Squadron Commander Capt. Reeder notified Cornell and his crew that repairs on another plane had been completed and it would be available for them to fly. Together the crew joyfully hitched a ride on a personnel carrier out to the repair hanger to check out their new ride. The crew arrived just as the repaired plane was being towed out of the hangar and were greeted with what must have been the oldest and, in Cornell's words, "junkiest" B-17 on the field. The plane was named "*Ol Dad*" and the crew felt that name was very appropriate. Cornell described his first impression of "*Ol Dad*":

"*The nose of our plane had a rather rakish figure of an old man painted on it shown with a large beer stein upraised in his hand. While I appreciated the art work, I could not help but notice that the airplane had about a thousand bullet holes and flak holes in it which were poorly patched. I later found that in flight these patches made melodious noises and that my placing my hands and feet over selected patches in the vicinity of the pilot's seat I could play a rough rendition of 'O Sole Mio'."*

Two days later on Saturday, March 18th, Cornell flew "*Ol' Dad*" on his first mission with his own crew. The mission was to bomb an airfield in southern Germany near Lechfield. Although they were again defended by P-51s, the group was repeatedly attacked by the German defenders on the way in and out of the target. Cornell observed a JU-88, just out of gun range, escorted by a force of ME-109s, firing a large experimental missile trailing smoke into his formation. The missile blew up near a P-51 and destroyed both the P-51 and a B-17 flying nearby. The crew was able to drop their bombs directly on the target on their first mission. The 100th Bomb Group lost a total of 3 planes but the mission was considered a success because of the accurate bomb placement by the entire group. Cornell's new ball turret gunner, John Pontzious, was credited with one enemy aircraft downed.

Not enough has been written about the extreme conditions that the bomber crews endured while flying on the six- to eight- hour missions in an unheated, unpressurized aircraft at altitudes of 20,000 to 30,000 feet. When the B-17 was designed in the early 1930s, aeronautical engineering had not yet developed the technology to build a fuselage to withstand the stresses of pressurization. For this reason, the crews were required to breathe through supplemental oxygen masks as the plane gained altitude. Even well-conditioned airmen begin to suffer from lack of oxygen at altitudes above 12,000 feet. The condition of hypoxia, or oxygen deprivation, gradually grows worse as the aircraft climbs higher. Each individual varies, of course, but studies have shown that at 15,000 feet, most aviators without added oxygen can only perform flying duties for 30 minutes or so before suffering from the effects of hypoxia. The condition of hypoxia is made even more dangerous by the fact that the gradual onset of oxygen deprivation may not be noticed at first. Some individuals may even become euphoric or not notice any symptoms at all until they are unable to make good decisions or worse, lose consciousness. The time of useful consciousness, defined as the amount of time an aviator can efficiently function without supplemental oxygen, varies with the altitude. At 22,000 feet, the time of useful consciousness ranges from 5 to 10 minutes, while at 30,000 feet the flyer has only 1 to 3 minutes to either add supplemental oxygen or immediately descend to a lower altitude.

On the B-17, oxygen was supplied by four separate independent systems to sixteen outlets throughout the plane and supplemented with portable bottles. Each crewmember was custom-fitted with an oxygen mask, which he was careful to keep adjusted and connected to the plane's outlet. At high altitudes, the dangers came from either the oxygen lines freezing up or being nicked by antiaircraft fire. And of course, since the bottles and the lines contained oxygen under high pressure, there was always an extreme fire hazard from severed or punctured lines that would spray flammable oxygen into the airplane. Because of these hazards, Cornell periodically had the crewmembers check in on the plane intercom to make sure they were still O.K.

One of Cornell's most vivid memories of the high-altitude missions was the constant, energy-sapping cold. At the operational altitudes that most strategic bombers flew, the outside air temperatures ranged from -20 to -50 degrees and this did not take into account the heat loss from moving air. Some heat was supplied to the cockpit by circulating glycol heated by the engine exhaust to take some of the sting out of the numbing cold, but none of this was available for the waist, ball turret, or tail gunners. The waist gunners suffered the most from the cold for in a battle they were standing at open bays next to the air stream with their machine guns. Their only heating was the electrical suit heaters in their wired underwear. Even then, just the touch of an ungloved hand on the airframe or gun meant frozen flesh or frostbite. B-17 crewmembers had to maintain top notch physical conditioning just to endure the effects of high altitude long missions, even without the dangers of enemy anti-aircraft fire and interceptors.

As soon as the aircrews landed they were picked up by a personnel carrier and transported directly to the Intelligence hut for debriefing. The debriefing officers wanted to get a record of the experiences and impressions of the crew while the mission was still fresh in their memory. While one of the officers went over the questions, sergeants and administrative personnel were filling out forms and taking copious notes. The debriefing officers specifically wanted the crew's opinion on bombing effectiveness, number and type of enemy planes, severity and location of antiaircraft fire, battle damage and any reports of enemy aircraft shot down or damaged. If any planes were lost within their unit, then additional reports were required about details of the loss, parachutes sighted, and any additional helpful information. All of this data would then be collated and sent to the squadron headquarters to be combined later with photographic interpretation of the results. Later, in the case of the loss of the bomber *"Ol' Dad"* with Cornell and his crew, a record of the debriefing of other crews in his squadron that made it back safely was maintained and located.

The second mission for Cornell's crew, and his third, was the "Big B" or Berlin. On Wednesday, March 22, 1944 a total of 460 B-17s and 196 B-24s from the 8th Force along with their fighter escorts took part in the mission. Their primary targets were the aviation plants at Oranienburg, but a cloud cover obscured the targets. So, they went to their secondary target, Berlin. Leading the 2nd Bomb Wing of B-24s was Maj. Jimmy Stewart, who was flying his 12th mission.

Stewart, who had earned his pilot's license in 1938 and his commercial license in 1939, had been drafted but failed to meet the weight requirements (he was too thin). Nevertheless he kept trying to build up his weight while volunteering and was finally accepted as a Private in March 1941, becoming the first major Hollywood star to enlist in the Army. Shortly after Pearl Harbor, he was commissioned and reassigned as a pilot. Sent to heavy bomber school and then used to create recruitment films, Stewart despaired of ever seeing combat. At age 35, he was considered too old to lead a fighting outfit. After appealing to his commanders, he was finally assigned to the 445th Bomb Group that flew B-24s. Arriving in England, the Group flew its first mission, to bomb the U-boat facilities in Kiel, Germany on Dec. 13th, 1943. Stewart was promoted to Major and awarded the Distinguished Flying Cross for actions as Deputy Commander of the 2nd Bomb Wing.

A constant cloud cover existed for most of the flight to Berlin and Cornell was worried that they would be unable to spot their target, but 30 miles from their target the clouds cleared and the crew was able to get their first sighting of the capitol of Germany. This time their fighter protection was able to stay with them all the way to the target and back. American P-38s, P-51s and P-47s were constantly circling over or to either side of the formation to attack any German interceptors that might appear. The bombers also delivered about 6 million leaflets to the citizens of Berlin.

Immediately after "Bombs Away!" the crew received a fright as "Ol' Dad" experienced a runaway propeller on their number two engine, shaking the wing violently. Runaway propellers, usually from a lack of oil pressure, are especially dangerous for the crew for if the propeller separates from the engine; there is a reasonable chance it will penetrate the cockpit area as it rips free from the crankshaft. Cornell had no choice but to reduce power to the other engines to reduce the vibration, reducing their airspeed to just above stalling. Consequently their plane began to lag behind the safety of the massed formation. Within moments, two P-47s appeared on both sides of their plane, but because of orders to maintain radio silence over Germany, Cornell was unable to tell them of his engine problems. Fortunately, the crankshaft finally broke on the number two engine, allowing the propeller to windmill harmlessly, so Cornell was able to again apply full power to the other three engines and regain most of his speed and altitude. The P-47s, seeing the plane regain speed, then left for other pastures. That day the 8th Air Force lost 7 B-17s and 5 B-24s due to the fierce antiaircraft fire concentrated around Berlin. However, none of Cornell's squadron lost any planes on this mission and the crew agreed that the runways at Thorpe-Abbots never looked prettier upon their tardy return.

Cornell marveled at the ability of the mechanics back at Thorpe Abbotts to replace an engine, patch over the flak holes, and keep *"Ol Dad"* ready for combat duty. Working most of the time outside in the weather, the mechanics would swarm over their plane, bringing out their tools and replacement parts to the concrete hardstand where the planes were parked. For some repairs, such as replacing whole panels or fuselage parts, the plane would be towed into one of the giant hangars. Many of the repairs would take place overnight if the missions were scheduled back to back, but if an engine were replaced the plane had to be first checked out with a "slow flight" before it could be flown on a mission. The gunners were responsible for cleaning and oiling their own guns.

A vital key to the concept of strategic bombing was the accurate placement of bombs directly on the target. However, accomplishing this proved to be much harder in actual practice than in theory. In the real world, many factors are involved in accuracy, including the altitude and speed of the airplane, wind drift, and attitude of the plane as the bomb leaves and perhaps most importantly, the training of the aircrews doing the bombing. By the 1920s it was clear that more had to be done to achieve the accuracy necessary if targets were to be destroyed by aerial bombing. The first to fund development work on an improved bombsight was the U.S. Navy. A Navy consultant, Carl L. Norden started working on the problem of accuracy and developed a gyro-stabilized system that became known as the Norden Bombsight. The Norden bombsight was in essence an analog computer that used the airplane's speed, altitude, wind drift, and an optical viewfinder to calculate the precise moment to drop the bomb. It was an extremely intricate device that required high precision manufacturing techniques so deliveries were slow in coming.

The first delivery was in 1931 and although the bombsight still had developmental problems, it was much more accurate than any other system. The Army Air Corps also requested the Norden Bombsight for all its planes. However, because of the friction between the services, the Navy refused to allow Norden to sell directly to the Air Corps, requiring instead that the Air Corps purchase the bombsight only through the Navy. Since the

Air Corps flew at greater altitudes and speed than the Navy, they needed modifications to the bombsight, but the Navy refused. Finally, in 1936 the Navy, afraid that they would not have enough bombsights for their own uses, canceled all deliveries to the Air Corps.

By this time the Norden Bombsight, which had been classified Top Secret, had gained a reputation for being able to "drop a bomb in a pickle barrel at 30,000 feet." This, of course, was not correct but the popular opinion boosted the morale of the Air Corps and lent credence to the theory of strategic bombing. Details about the bombsight were classified Top Secret and when the war began, bombardiers had to remove the bombsight when they left the plane.

At the same time, the Sperry Gyroscope Company had also been working on a gyroscopically stabilized bombsight. When the Air Corps learned of this, they turned instead to Sperry to manufacture their bombsights, although conceding that the Norden was more accurate. The Air Corps began to install some Sperry bombsights in their bombers, but finally in 1943 the Navy, realizing that it had too many bombsights, allowed the Air Corps to use their surplus. The Sperry contracts were cancelled and the Air Corps was finally able to obtain all the Norden bombsights they needed. To achieve maximum effectiveness, the bomber pilot had to fly absolutely straight and level during the final seconds before the bomb was released, so the later versions included an autopilot that controlled the plane from the bombardier's station. Of course, the most dangerous phase of the bombing run was just before "bombs away," so antiaircraft gunners quickly learned to fire their utmost when the bomb bay doors opened.

Although their plane was constantly hit by fragments of exploded aerial bursts, the crew of *"Ol Dad"* luckily did not suffer any major injuries on its long missions. Other crews were not so lucky, returning many times with injured, bleeding, or dead crewmembers on board.   Cornell's tail gunner, Hugh Hamilton, never mentioned until long after the war his injury:

"The only time I got hit by enemy fire, I was lucky. Explanation: my parachute – a chest pack with two big snaps – was behind me, out of my way.   Over my fleece-lined clothes, I wore the parachute harness, with two rings in front; a big metal buckle in front, also. We always wore a flak vest over everything – with strips of heavy metal inside it.   When I got hit, I was leaning forward.   A piece of flak came up between my knees, up between the flak vest and parachute harness.   It was as big as my thumb – it hit the buckle; the vest kept it from going out, so it went in through my clothes and imbedded in my stomach muscles.   It didn't really hurt – I don't think – but when we were out of danger, I reached in to get it.   Felt a few drops of dried blood.   Didn't mention it to anyone.   Didn't want a Purple Heart for something insignificant."

Cornell's plane was loaded mostly with 500 and 1,000 pound aerial bombs to drop.   In order to transport and load the bombs safely, the bombs were not actually armed until the plane was well on the way to its target. The fuze on the front of each bomb was set off by a striker pin, but the striker pin was blocked by a clockwork mechanism. A tiny propeller on the front of the bomb turned as the bomb dropped, rotating the clockwork mechanism to free the firing pin. A cotter pin blocked the propeller so it could not turn on the ground or while being loaded or in flight, thus making the bomb unable–in most cases–to explode. One of the tasks of the bombardier was to climb back into the bomb bay when it appeared the plane could reach its target, and pull out the cotter pin and replace them with a wire connected to the plane. When the bomb dropped away from the plane, the wire pulled free and released the propeller, which would turn an internal mechanism to clear the firing pin. When the bomb hit its target, the firing pin drove into the detonator, which exploded the bomb. The bombardier was tasked with retaining the pulled cotter pins and turning them in after the flight to prove that the bombs were armed and ready when they dropped. Cornell recalled that the bombardier was in deep trouble during debriefing if he came back without the full set of cotter pins as proof the bombs were armed. He heard through the grapevine that most prudent bombardiers maintained an extra set of cotter pins in case they had forgotten their duty in the middle of all the excitement. In case the mission was cancelled and the plane was ordered to turn back, the bombardier would go back and re-insert the cotter pins so they could land safely.

The aircrews, under the constant pressure of ongoing missions, were given time off whenever their schedule permitted.   However, even on leave they were reminded that a desperate war was being waged:

"We had occasional three-day leaves to settle our nerves a bit and everybody seemed to head to London en masse.   I tagged along but if I had given it much thought I would have surely preferred to ride my new bike (everybody had one) around the quiet English countryside and examine the ancient buildings. . . It was during one of these leaves in London that we heard an unusually loud explosion with the usual results of the building shaking, plaster falling down and general confusion.   It turned out later that this was the first of the V-1 missile barrage."

By the spring of 1944, the 8th Air Force was conducting missions deep within Germany whenever the weather allowed, striking at airports, factories, and oil refineries.   On March 23, 1944, Cornell's crew was part of a force of 524 B-17s and 244 B-24s sent to Brunswick, Germany to bomb aircraft factories. Although the mission was partially satisfactory, the force lost 16 B-17s with 9 casualties and 158 missing in action. With Doolittle's new policy on fighter protection, they were accompanied all the way to Brunswick and back by P-38s, P-47s, and P-51s. Sometimes the roles of "little friends" and the big bombers were reversed. On the return from this mission, a twin-engined P-38 escort was deep in enemy territory when one engine got hit with anti-aircraft and the pilot had to shut it down.   Right then the huge formation of massed B-17 gunners looked very inviting. Cornell remembered:

"With one engine inoperative, he was incapable of defending himself and he must have stung the Germans

pretty good because they were surely hot after him. Every
time they made an attack he would slide up under the other
side of a B-17 squadron (normally, six aircraft) giving him
the protection of our guns. After some minutes of this hair-
pulling routine the Germans gave up and returned home
and our lame duck "little friend" left us."

With the exception of one crewmember who was
hit by a fragment of flak in the heel of his shoe, *"Ol' Dad"*
was proving to be a reliable, if noisy and drafty, war horse.
On 11 April 1944 Cornell's crew participated on a mission
to bomb the Heinkel Aircraft factory in Rostock, Germany.
Out of his group of 302 B-17s sent out, 33 were shot down
with a loss of 330 men killed, wounded, or POWs.

Cornell kept a close lookout on his crew members
for signs of distress due to the constant pressure of
combat flying almost daily. Because of the common mess
halls and airman's and officer's barracks, everyone was
aware of the empty spaces when a crew failed to return.
Even before a mission debriefing was finished most
everyone learned about the number of planes lost and the
crewmembers missing. Some of his crew refused to talk
about it, while others took refuge in alcohol while a few
tried to sleep as much as possible. Cornell observed the
range of human emotion as the crew grappled with the
daily task facing their death in the skies. He was proud of
the fact that every single member of his crew refused to go
on sick call and showed up every morning–even with an
occasional hangover– to climb back into the bomber. The
daily reduction of crewmembers was matched by the

arrival of green replacement crews and Cornell saw himself in every new pilot who checked into the base.

Every mission had its heart-pounding moments and on one long mission across the North Sea, Denmark, and the Baltic, "*Ol' Dad's*" number two engine began spewing oil out of the breather on top of the engine under the cowl flap just after they crossed the Danish Coast. Since this was a clear indication of an internal engine failure, and the long mission ahead required all four engines developing full power, Cornell had no choice but to shut down the engine, abort the mission, and return to base. This of course meant leaving the protection of the massed group and the accompanying fighters and returning to base alone, so Cornell dropped down several thousand feet and tried to stay in a thick layer of stratus clouds as much as possible on the way back to Thorpe Abbotts. Lt. Tennenbaum charted a course straight back to their home base as they returned alone. Luckily, they did not cross any German fighter planes on their way back.

Immediately after landing, Cornell was summoned to report immediately to the Commanding Officer, Lt. Col. Bennett. He reported in still clad in his heavy flying gear and was startled to be treated rather brusquely by his commander because Cornell had aborted the mission. Shortly thereafter, a mechanic arrived at the office and verified the facts of the failing engine, thereby justifying Cornell's decision to abort. Nevertheless, Cornell felt that his judgement as an aircraft commander had been questioned and it stung:

"I know that our commanders had the world's toughest jobs and I want to be charitable but he could have handled the whole thing better. . . before the evidence was all in."

By this time most missions were composed of up to 1,000 planes from the 8th Air Force alone, not counting the fighters, and on virtually every mission Cornell's crew witnessed one or more B-17s in death throes, some from direct hits from antiaircraft fire or other sources:

"These usually exploded making a tragic and spectacular scenario. We did not normally wear our chest pack at all times, they were much too bulky and interfered with out duties at all stations. We wore our harness to which the parachute could be quickly attached when danger appeared to be imminent. Thus when an aircraft exploded without warning there was a great deal of debris thrown about in all directions including the bodies of the occupants. . . The engines would continue in a forward direction much like the extended, palm down, fingers of the hand in a gentle ever-downward curve, the props providing a gyroscopic influence which kept them on a more or less even course, and the engines appeared to be still running - this being pure speculation, of course."

Although in the spring of 1944 the 8th Air Force bomber crews, including Cornell and his crew, were not privy to the plans for the upcoming invasion of the European mainland, they were aware that their missions began to include railroad marshalling yards and suspected missile-launching sites in France. In the mess halls and the repair shops scuttlebutt had it that "D-Day" was fast approaching. On April 27, all the crews of the 100th Bomb Group were scheduled to fly a very early morning mission to France, which relieved the crews because they felt these missions were less hazardous than the long missions deep within Germany. After arising, being briefed, and eating long before daylight, Cornell and the crew were dropped off at their plane for their twelfth (and Cornell's 13th) mission:

"On arrival at my B-17, 'O' Dad' number 3543, I discovered that my chest pack parachute had been removed for repacking which was done every sixty days. . .frankly, I had obtained an extra chute in some covert operation and stored it under my seat. Rather than walk a half a mile back to Supply for another chute I decided to use my spare for this relatively easy mission and beside, I was not going to be shot down today, anyway, RIGHT? This spare chute had not been repacked for a lengthy time and was liberally covered with oil and the like from maintenance work in the vicinity."

The usual procedure for the forming up the group was takeoffs at minimum distance apart and climbing through any cloud layers to assemble at altitude over the local radio station. Many times in climbing through the clouds on instruments, Cornell's plane was buffeted by prop wash from a nearby plane, indicating that they had just missed colliding with another bomber in the clouds. Assembling 1,000 heavily laden bombers in one section of the sky to depart en masse was a nerve racking ordeal, and doing so before daylight was even more so. The mission went as planned and the crew found clear weather at the bombing target. Cornell remembered:

"After 'bombs away' over the missile site we had an easy descending flight path back to our base, arriving, I think, before noon. Only recently the number of missions in a tour of duty had been increased from twenty-five to thirty. We counted ourselves fortunate to have twelve out of the way and thirteen for me. Upon landing we were informed that we should not relax too much as we were going right back out again. This time it would be an airfield in the corner of Germany, France, and Luxembourg by the name of Thionville. After gassing, loading, and taking off plus the usual defensive assembly, we made our target but were prevented by bombing by a bothersome little cloud deck over the airdrome. So we pressed on to our alternate target in southern Belgium by the name of Le Colot airfield."

Their bomb bay doors were open and the plane was on autopilot waiting for their bombs to drop when the first round of anti-aircraft fire blew away the number four engine. The second round hit the number three engine and the third round exploded near the open bomb bay doors. Their long day just got much longer.

*   *   *   *   *

When Aircraft number 42-3534 piloted by 1st Lt. Winans C. Shaddix failed to return to Thorpe Abbotts, the other returning aircrews went through their usual post-mission debriefing and a Missing Air Crew Report (MACR) was filed on their missing comrades. Members of Cornell's squadron were interviewed and statements taken from the last squadron members to have sighted the plane. The official report (MACR #04268) listed all the pertinent details about Cornell and his crew, the date and time of the final sighting, and gave the following summary of the incident:

"A/C #534 was hit by flak as it left the target area (Le Culot A/D) at 1939 hours. No. 3 engine began to smoke and the A/C began to lag. It remained with the formation, however, until 2110 hours when 10 chutes were seen to come out, and the A/C descended in slow spirals, apparently under AFCE control. (Capt. Van Steenis, Lt. McGuire, Lt. Harris)"

The reference to "apparently under AFCE control" refers to Automatic Flight Control Equipment, an early form of autopilot, which would have tried to stabilize the airplane after the crew bailed out. Of course no autopilot could compensate for two missing engines on one wing, hence the slow spiral downward.

The filing of a Missing Air Crew Report triggered a series of events, mostly sad and immediately necessary. First, an administrative sergeant was tasked with the unenviable job of going to the Nissen Hut where Cornell, Sullivan, and Dailey slept and boxing up their belongings. He made sure to get any boots under the bunk and clothes hanging at the end. Carefully he combed the hut to insure that no trace of the missing men's belongings would be left so it could be made ready for the next occupants. Later that day he did the same for the enlisted men who bunked together in another hut. Cornell's bicycle was donated to the maintenance shop to be used to cover the mile-long dispersal parking areas. Then another sergeant went carefully through the boxes to insure that anything that contained military secrets (mission details, etc.) or embarrassing to the family was removed. The boxes were then sealed and addressed to be shipped to the airman's listed next-of-kin.

But first, 9 telegrams had to be written and sent to the nearest relative. In notifying the next-of-kin of wounded, deceased, or captured soldiers, the War Department normally attempted to quickly gather what details were available and transmit them to the nearest relatives as soon as possible. In the case of Cornell, his hometown of Double Springs did not have a telegraph office, so the telegram went to the nearest Western Union office at Jasper, Alabama. When the telegram printed out, it came with the code for "Report Delivery", meaning that the deliverer had to have someone from the household sign a receipt form that was sent back immediately to the War Department, proving that the family had been notified. The telegram was sealed in a standard envelope requesting a signature and hand carried the two blocks to the U.S. Post Office. The delivery was made the following morning by a rural postman who guessed at the contents, since he had delivered similarly marked envelopes before. At the Shaddix home, instead of putting the mail in the mailbox out on the roadside, he drove carefully up the driveway, got out of his car and walked slowly to the front porch. When Cornell's mother answered the door, he handed her the envelope and thrust forward a form to be signed, offering her his pen. She did not understand at first, but signed the offered form and then opened the envelope. It contained the standard wording in such cases:

"THE SECRETARY OF WAR DESIRES ME TO EXPRESS HIS DEEP REGRET THAT YOUR SON 1ST LT. WINANS C. SHADDIX HAS BEEN MISSING IN ACTION SINCE 27 APRIL 1944. IF FURTHER DETAILS OR OTHER INFORMATION IS RECEIVED YOU WILL BE PROMPTLY NOTIFIED."

Chapter 5

Victor and the Maquis

On 11 April 1944 while Cornell and his crew were being awakened early for a mission to bomb the Heinkel Aircraft factory in Rostock, Germany, a dull black Handley Page 4-engined Halifax bomber from RAF Tempsford in England took off a few hours earlier on a secret mission to France. The fuselage of the Halifax bomber had been modified to carry personnel and cargo thus the bomb bay doors were replaced with an enlarged hatch so that containers of supplies and paratroopers could exit the aircraft while in flight. The bomber crew was experienced in navigating across France in the night, and this mission was not much different from the ones that had gone before. Two squadrons of aircraft, the 138th and 161st RAF, specialized in dropping Special Operations agents and supplies mostly during the eight moonlit nights around the full moon. Their missions were kept a top secret and even very few Britons ever knew of the nature and destination of their cargo. Hitler himself knew that the aircraft were all coming out of one base, but his military intelligence section was never able to pinpoint the exact location. He reportedly said ". . . find this viper's nest and obliterate it." In all, 995 Special Ops agents and resistance fighters were dropped into enemy occupied Europe before D-Day but at the cost of 126 aircraft that failed to return, many of the crews and the agents they were carrying being killed.

Reducing their altitude and flying slowly over the target drop zone; the Halifax located the proper coordinates near the border of Belgium and France and flew multiple passes at a low altitude searching for a flashlight signal. At the appointed place and time, a blinking light from the ground was sighted, so the Halifax circled back around to where the lights had blinked and slowed to just above its stalling airspeed. The area below them was mountainous and covered with forests, so the spot selected had to be in a small cleared area on top of a gentle rise. Luckily, there was almost no wind, so if they dropped their cargo accurately, it should come down in the correct general area. The drop crew stood near the open hatch door waiting for the amber light to change to green. When the light flashed green, they quickly pushed five containers with attached parachutes out the door.

The containers held weapons, ammunition, food, and tents. The army had experimented with the best containers for dropping supplies and found that heavy canvas padded cylinders similar to a long duffel bag with either felt or cardboard liners worked best. The containers came in several sizes according to the load and were laced with woven straps to connect to the parachute. The aerial delivery parachute, known as type G-1, was a 24' canopy for use with loads up to 300 pounds. It was developed and tested before the war by the U.S. Army Material Command and standardized in December of 1942.

The green light was extinguished as the Halifax left the area and made a wide sweeping turn to again approach the drop zone while three men gathered near the open hatch. When the light flashed green again, the three parachutists stepped out of the hatch one by one and disappeared into the darkness below. Only one of the men had paratrooper training; the other two men had made just three jumps before this one but none of them in the dark. The pilot added power, gained altitude and began his return to Tempsford. One more mission down, still many to go.

Two of the parachutists were from France and the third was an American. The Frenchmen were Maj. Jacques Bollardière of the French army in exile in England and a radio operator Gerard Brault. The third one was Lt. Victor Layton of the American OSS. Their mission was to connect with a group of resistance fighters located in the Ardennes Forest and try to equip and organize a small guerilla band to help delay the Germans rushing to the coast on D-Day.

Prior to World War II, the United States did not have a central coordinating intelligence agency or even a comprehensive foreign intelligence gathering policy. Part of the problem was an inherent distaste for spying on others. In the words of one government official in 1929, "Gentlemen do not read each other's mail." Because of this outlook, the Navy, the War Department, the State Department, and the FBI all quietly conducted their own intelligence gathering and none of the agencies were very forthcoming to share their findings with the other agencies. The Navy had the Office of Naval Intelligence (ONI), which was woefully underfunded and understaffed, as was the War Department's Military Intelligence Division (MID). The FBI was mostly concerned with investigations within the borders of the United States. The State Department was privy to much information in the course of going about their daily business, but the diplomats were mostly instructed to abstain from actual spying activities.

In addition to this, another part of the problem was the lack of any formal or written procedures within the government for the coordination and dissemination of useful data that might be found. The separate departments seemed more interested in guarding their own empires than in sharing information that they had gathered. As President Roosevelt became more aware of the dangers of these obstacles to intelligence, he began in 1939 to urge the agencies to work together and come up with some sort of coordinating body.

The British, on the other hand, had a long history of active and successful intelligence gathering. As far back as the turn of the century the Secret Service Bureau conducted foreign espionage and counter-espionage. Developed in a hot bed of European communities, the Bureau collected and analyzed military and commercial intelligence. Their methods were refined during World War I and further codified in the period between the wars. The top military officers felt their survival depended upon knowing the intentions and abilities of all the warring powers. Their Directorate of Military Intelligence (DMI) combined all the aspects of information gathering, code breaking, counterintelligence, and liaison with other agencies to become an effective weapon in their national survival. They were aghast at the indifference shown by the United States military toward spying and urged President Roosevelt at every chance to organize the scattered and quarreling agencies toward greater efficiency in gathering and using intelligence information.

Finally in July 1941 the president announced the creation of a new agency, the Coordination of Information (COI) to become the first peacetime national intelligence-gathering body. It was charged with the authority to "collect an analyze all information and data which may bear upon the national security." In addition, the COI was to act as a central organization to disseminate the collected information to all pertinent officials. This announcement was met, however, with almost instant opposition from the feuding agencies who saw this newcomer as a threat to their traditional prerogatives. This opposition continued throughout the war and greatly hampered the efforts of the U.S. to centralize intelligence gathering and dissemination.

The man President Roosevelt chose to lead the new agency, former assistant U.S. Attorney General William J. Donovan, was an ideal choice. Donovan, a veteran of World War I, had been an inspiring leader who had been awarded the Congressional Medal of Honor for his bravery and exploits on the battlefield. But more importantly, Donovan was a charismatic leader who searched for the best practices of other spy agencies, recruited some of the most unusual soldiers and creative scientists, and adopted innovative techniques to train and equip his troops for the realities of all out war. "Wild Bill," as he became known, was a realistic diplomat who could work with the allies and listen to their suggestions. He possessed a rare ability to absorb information quickly, adapt when necessary, and persuade others of his viewpoint.

The events at Pearl Harbor and the entry of the U.S. into the war soon shifted the traditional relationships. Donovan, after becoming aware of the damaging nature of the inter-service rivalries, realized that to be truly effective, the COI would need to work closer with the newly formed Joint Chiefs of Staff, so he proposed to bring the coordinating agency under their jurisdiction. The President agreed, so on June 13 1942 the COI's name was changed to the Office of Strategic Services (OSS) and the new organization was folded into the military.

Taking cues from the British, the OSS quickly began to adopt many of their best practices and concepts. Donovan held that, "In war it is the results that count, and the saboteurs and guerrilla leaders in Special Operations and the Operational Groups, the spies in Secret Intelligence, and the radio operators in Communications did produce some impressive results." In this unconventional warfare "persuasion, penetration, and intimidation are the modern counterparts of sapping and mining in the siege warfare of former days"

The newly created OSS was truly unlike any other government agency that had been created in the past or the present. Donovan recruited widely from the Ivy League colleges, from law firms and business groups, and from foreign governments such as the British MI9. From this beginning Donovan began to lead the OSS to conduct a "shadow war" that recognized none of the past boundaries. Most of the recruits were young and many did not have a military background. Above all, the recruiters were told to look for individuals who possessed "out-of-the-box" thinking and the ability to come up with novel solutions.

At the same time Donovan and his team began to search widely for recruits who spoke multiple languages, who had lived abroad, or who had traveled extensively abroad. They accepted American citizens, recent immigrants, ex-POWs with local knowledge, and anyone who they thought might conceivably help them penetrate the enemy defenses and bring back information. However, the other Defense Department agencies did not cease their objections to a central intelligence-gathering agency or willingly share their information. Instead, they continued to obstruct the efforts of the OSS and use their influence to diminish its capabilities.

The OSS established "spy schools" first in Canada and then later in Maryland near what is now Camp David. The schools were organized along the British system with spymasters who taught research and analysis, morale operations (propaganda), counter-espionage, special operations (for sabotage and guerilla warfare) and operational groups (highly trained foreign-language-speaking commando teams). The training exercises the school developed proved to be so effective they are continued to this day with the CIA and the Army Special Forces.

For the teams that were going to be dropped behind enemy lines, the OSS developed an extensive counterfeiting operation to produce forged documents that would withstand any scrutiny. They purchased the finest printers and hired former employees of the government printing office to set up shop a block away from OSS headquarters in London. They procured originals to copy, developed and produced the proper type of paper, and even purchased the original German inks from a company in neutral Switzerland. The printed forgeries were mechanically abraded and aged to appear worn and wrinkled. In the end, the forgeries were so exact that even experts could not tell the difference. The OSS even went to great extremes to provide the operatives with the type of clothing normally found in the area they were sent. They obtained these clothes from many sources, including purchasing them right off the backs of puzzled newly arrived refugees. They made sure the agent's shoes were of the type generally worn in that area and were made of the correct type of treated leather. Nothing that would betray the origin of the team member was left to chance.

In 1943 in preparation for D-Day, the OSS began a multi-pronged effort to assist the invasion forces in Europe. They created forces that would work behind the front lines to delay and obstruct the German Army from moving quickly to the Normandy coast, to rally and organize the guerilla and underground fighters, and to cause as much confusion and damage as possible to the German defenders to aid the invading Allies.

As part of these preparations for D-Day, the OSS joined with the British Special Operations Section and the French Intelligence agency in exile and established a clandestine Operational Group (OG) training center near Jedburgh, Scotland. Known as the "Jedburgh Operation," this was the first serious cooperative effort from all the Allies to combine the assets of each intelligence agency. The French and British agencies were quick to recognize and appreciate the huge influx of supplies by the Americans. Beginning in 1943, the OSS combed the ranks of the U.S. Army for men who spoke French, were physically fit, and would volunteer for a hazardous assignment behind enemy lines. The operation, as could have been predicted, attracted an unusual group of men. The American and British who volunteered were mostly adventurers, rough-and-ready types who were bored with regular training missions, ex-paratroopers, and some intellectuals. The French volunteers were mostly former officers from the French army in exile. For some of them, this was the only way they could get back to their former country and directly engage with the invading Germans. But all of them were made aware of a not-so-secret order that Hitler had issued on 18 October 1942 to the Gestapo:" . . . *all enemies on commando missions, even if they are in uniform, armed or unarmed, in battle or flight, are to be slaughtered to the last man. . . If it should be necessary to spare one man or two, for interrogations, then they are to be shot immediately after this is completed."* Thus the OSS operatives realized that capture by the Germans would mean almost certain death after a very unpleasant interrogation. For this reason all of the commandos were issued a "suicide" pill along with their normal survival gear of maps, compass, French francs, and weapons. Several graduates of the Jedburgh School went on to greater responsibility, including William Colby, who parachuted into France in August 1944 and earned a Silver Star for his work with the underground. Colby later joined the Central Intelligence Agency and served as the station chief for the CIA in Saigon during the Vietnam conflict. After a long career in the CIA, Colby was chosen to lead the agency in 1971. During the time he was the director of the CIA he led many reform efforts to modernize the agency,

The planned Operational Groups were made up of three man teams consisting of a commanding officer, an executive officer, and a non-commissioned radio operator.

One of the officers would be from the country in which the operation would take place. The teams were trained in demolitions, hand-to-hand combat, Morse code, and taught the basics of parachuting. Their initial training took place in the highlands of Scotland, but for parachute training they transferred to the British parachute school at RAF Ringway, on the outskirts of Manchester, England. Their training schedule was so tight they were able to only get in three jumps at 500 feet to prepare them for their upcoming mission, before they were transferred to their final training at Milton Hall near Peterborough, England. Here they were allowed to spend more time to get to know each other and to choose their individual members of their team. Given time to get to become better acquainted, most teams were formed on the basis of personal friendship and professional fitness. After the teams were chosen, they received more training in guerrilla tactics, sabotage and evasion techniques and codes and communications and learned to work together as teams.

The radio operators were trained to transmit their codes on an innovative early portable radio, which had been developed by the OSS as a clandestine high frequency receiver, transmitter, and power supply that was typically carried in a "suitcase." According to one historian, the units were designed so that they could fit within a typical European loaf of bread. The radio was designed, as much as possible for that time, to be serviceable in rough environments and could operate either on 120/220 volts AC or a 6-volt dry cell battery. The radio could also be powered by a hand-cranked generator that the OSS had developed. The range could be up to 300 miles if an antenna were attached.

The goals of the Jedburgh units were many: after parachuting into occupied France behind the enemy lines, they were to establish contact with the local Resistance fighters and to interrupt the German supply lines, delay their movement of troops, and to sabotage factories, fuel dumps, and power plants. They would transmit regularly scheduled reports by Morse code using their portable radios. The radios could also be used to schedule supply drops of ammunition, weapons, and food. Their tactics were to conduct guerilla-type hit-and-run raids but not try to seize and hold territory.

These OSS operations were directly under the control of General Eisenhower, who, in planning for the invasion, was concerned with the Germans swiftly moving their troops forward to the invasion beaches and stopping the invasion on the beachhead. On 22 March 1944 General Eisenhower stated in a secret memo, "We are going to need very badly the support of the Resistance groups in France." Prior to this, the OSS had suffered a chronic lack of respect and funding from the top brass of the Army. This statement by the Supreme Commander, Allied Expeditionary Headquarters (SHAEF) solidified the support for the efforts of the OSS at least for the upcoming invasion. It allowed the OSS to obtain a larger allocation of aircraft and the supplies it badly needed to send along with the insertion units. It also gave the OSS a higher priority in scheduling aircraft drop missions for their secret agents.

To isolate the landing beaches, the Allies planned a series of attacks and maneuvers behind the enemy lines by airborne commandos, OSS special teams, and local partisans. Eisenhower felt that if he could delay the Germans rushing their reserve forces to the landing beaches, he could use the delay to offload more men, artillery, and supplies to secure his foothold.

Rommel, on the other hand, knew that he did not have enough troops to adequately defend every inch of the entire coast of France against an invasion in strength. So he made the decision to place part of his units as coastal defenses and maintain a reserve of strength some miles back from the coast to rush to the site of actual invasion. He placed his highly mobile units, the Panzer Divisions, in the rear across from the narrowest point in the English Channel, the Straits of Dover. In this manner he hoped to throw the invaders back into the sea before they gained a secure foothold on the beach. Of course this plan depended upon accurately identifying the actual invasion location, good communications from his frontline troops to his rearward reserves, and quick deployment of his mobile units to the front lines.

Major Jacques Paris de Bollardière, the leader of the team who parachuted from the Halifax on 11 April 1944, was a graduate of the Military Academy at Saint-Cyr in 1930. He went on active service and transferred to the Foreign Legion in 1935, where he served in Algeria until the war started. He returned to the French homeland to fight the German invaders. Compact in build with a shock of straight black hair, he wore thick corrective lenses and was absolutely fearless. When France fell, he refused to surrender and instead escaped to England where he joined the Free French Forces and vowed to continue to fight in any capacity. The collaborationist Vichy Regime sentenced him to death in absentia. He was posted to North Africa and fought with the British forces in the 1st Free French Division in the East Africa campaign mostly against the Italians. He was promoted to Major and awarded the Cross of the Liberation and next took part in the battle of El Alamein. Here he was so severely wounded in the arm and shoulder by an exploding artillery shell that he spent eight months in a hospital recuperating. When he was released, he returned to England and volunteered again in 1943 for Special Forces training and went through paratrooper training in order to go on a mission behind enemy lines in France. He was appointed head of "Mission Citronelle," which was a Special Operations mission to parachute into the Ardennes area and organize and lead a guerilla army in anticipation of the Allied invasion of Europe.

The second Frenchman, Gerard Brault, was also a very determined fighter. Born in Paris in 1922, the slightly built Brault had joined the resistance while still a student at a technical school. When the resistance leader Jean Moulin was parachuted back into France to try to unite the feuding resistance groups, he needed constant radio contact with the OSS. One of his main radio operators was Brault, who operated an underground radio transmitter/receiver in Paris in 1943 for Moulin. The Gestapo, using radio transmission tracking equipment, finally managed to zero in on Brault's transmitter in his apartment in Paris. He was captured, tortured, and imprisoned but managed to escape, finally making his way to England in early 1944. While there he volunteered to make use of his radio skills and go back into France, but initially the British refused to send him, stating that his face was well known to the Gestapo. He voluntarily underwent cosmetic surgery to alter his appearance so the British gave in and made him a part of Mission Citronelle. He was trained to operate and maintain the OSS portable radio.

The third man who parachuted out of the Halifax that night was an American with an unusual background, Lt. Victor J. Layton. Born Victor Lustig in Vienna, Austria on November 28, 1921, the son of a banker, Victor was seven years old when his father was transferred to another bank in Paris, France. Because of these childhood residences, Victor grew up speaking both German and French as a native. At the age of 15 Victor's parents sent him to England for further schooling, where he became fluent in English. An excellent student, Victor was studying Engineering in 1940 when the war started. He made his way first to Spain, then sneaked aboard a Portuguese trawler bound for the United States. There he finished his education and changed his last name from Lustig, which to him sounded too Germanic, to Layton. He became a U.S. citizen and enlisted in the Army in 1942 and was commissioned a 2nd Lieutenant in the Army Engineers. Of slender build with thick, wavy black hair,

Victor had the looks of a Hollywood idol but the good looks belied a quick-thinking mind and a daring nature.

Lt. Victor Layton, OSS

In 1943 when the OSS was combing the ranks of the U.S. Army for soldiers who were multi-lingual, Lt. Layton's name popped up. Not only was he fluent in French, he spoke German as a native and had actually lived in both countries. The OSS had found a perfect match for its unusual requirements. He was quickly transferred from the Army Engineers to the OSS and shipped to London. He, too, was transferred to the training camp near Jedburgh, Scotland and became a Special Operations officer. During the training sessions he became friends with Major Bollardière and Gerard Brault. Together they volunteered to go as a group and try to organize the French Resistance fighters in the Ardennes area.

Even with the hazards of a nighttime drop into a heavily wooded area, all three parachutists landed without injury. When they reached the ground they found the resistance fighters had already gathered up the airdropped supplies, and were waiting on the Commandant to arrive. Maj. Bollardière introduced himself by his code name "Prism," and presented Lt. Layton as "Triad," and radioman Brault as "Senegal." Thereafter they would always go by these code names. The new arrivals emptied the airdropped containers and inspected the contents for damage. One of the canisters had snagged in the top of a tree, but it was being retrieved as the men gathered. The canisters contained American M1 rifles and a few Colt automatic pistols with ammunition, explosives, medical supplies, K-rations, French francs, and most importantly, the radio. It had been packed in a special canister with a crushable bottom section of corrugated cardboard. Radio operator Brault did not rest until he had assembled the radio, installed the proper crystal, and using a dry cell battery, tried it out by sending a message back to the Special Force headquarters in London. Shortly thereafter, the group gathered anxiously around the set heard the all-important dah-dah-dit of the Morse code receiver. The OSS leaders in London knew of the team's arrival long before the Halifax bomber got back to Tempsford. The accompanying supplies gave the arriving team instant credibility to the French Resistance fighters, who had a few single shot bolt-action French rifles.

The Resistance fighters that met the new arrivals were clad in civilian clothes but most were wearing a version of the Basque beret with a circular badge attached. They referred to themselves as Maquis, or French for "the bush," the scrub growth of thickets that covered parts of mountains where they lived. The local populace often called the guerillas "the Marquisards", or armed resistance fighters, a term that came to symbolize the entire French resistance network. Before the arrival of Maj. Bollardière and his men, the Maquis could listen to coded messages broadcast on BBC radio, but they had no way of sending back important information regarding German troop movements or unit strengths. The arrival of the new team and the supplies meant they could step up their attacks on German outposts and coordinate with other resistance groups.

One of the first tasks Maj. Bollardière had to accomplish was to get a quick survey of the enemy forces he was facing, their numbers and armament, and specific locations. He found that the local German units had learned to not patrol the craggy hills unless they came in force, for small squads or pairs would be spotted and overwhelmed by the Maquis. Most of the time the Germans withdrew back to fortified compounds at night. The Maquis, on the other hand, did most of their traveling to obtain food and ammunition at night, remaining in the secluded highland camps during the day. Thus they had been able to mount individual forays to harass the German outposts and damage their installations, always withdrawing quickly to avoid a pitched battle. The presence of three German outposts within a day's walking distance made their position precarious, for the German commanders had been warned that an invasion of the mainland by the Allies was imminent. One of the major advantages that the newcomers possessed was their radio communications and the fact that they could arrange for the arrival of more guns, explosives, ammunition, and money. This fact was not lost on the local Maquis.

After the three landed, over the next several days the number of volunteers to the local Maquis swelled from an original estimate of about 20 until over 200 showed up looking to join. Maj. Bollardière and Lt. Layton quickly organized training exercises to try to mold the volunteers into a fighting outfit. However, their initial supply of weapons and supplies were inadequate for the deluge of men. Frantically they radioed OSS headquarters for more guns and ammunition, but London was swamped with the details of the upcoming invasion of the mainland, and all available aircraft were being used on previously planned missions. They did receive one night drop but it was already scheduled to provide sleeping bags, explosives and more medicines. What was needed more urgently was more rifles and ammo. The new Commander did what he could with the limited weapons and supplies.

The Major and his crew sought out local families who supported their mission and those who were sympathetic. They enlisted some of these family members who were willing to serve as the "eyes and ears" for the operation. One of these families, the Fontaines, furnished both information and home-cooked meals to the newcomers. They were dining with the Fontaine family on 5 June 1944 when Lt. Layton "Triad" rose to speak to the group. Interviewed in 2010, still in her original home when she was 83, their daughter Georgette recalled:

"Lieutenant Victor was sitting there, ... He was a handsome man. He always looked at his watch. He stood up. And he said 'My dear friends the landing is imminent. At a time when I talk it's probably done.' A bomb could have fallen in the room . . it would not have caused the same dramatic effect."

What happened next is shrouded in controversy. What is known is that just after the invasion of the European mainland on 6 June 1944, a wave of euphoria swept over Occupied France, and especially among the Maquis, as the people could envision the end of their crippling occupation by the Germans. A piercing rain fell for several days in the Ardennes Mountains where the Maquis were camping. They erected several tents made from the supply parachutes and a fire was kept burning. There were reports that an aircraft bearing a German swastika flew overhead. Nevertheless, on 12 June 1944 a German unit formed from the ranks of 36th Panzer Regiment, recently arrived from the Russian front, made a determined effort to locate and destroy the resistance fighters in the mountains. The Germans may have been tipped off by some local collaborators or may have been acting on information by the aerial spotter, but they concentrated a force of nearly 3,000 veteran troops backed with armored vehicles near the town of Revin to confront the Maquis. In the battle that ensued, Maj. Bollardière realized that the Germans were in the process of making flanking maneuvers on both sides to encircle his men, so he ordered a retreat. He and Lt. Layton led a charge through a hail of bullets to escape with some of the men, but half of the young recruits froze and stayed behind. Shortly afterward their ammunition was expended and they were completely surrounded and overwhelmed. A total of 106 of the Maquis surrendered to the attacking Germans, almost all of whom had just joined the Maquis in the heady days after D-day.

In the evening of that same day, all the prisoners were beaten and shot, mostly in groups of five, in a massacre that lasted almost two hours. Not a one of the prisoners was left alive. The bodies were hastily buried in pits nearby at a place called "The Father of Oak", but later on 21 June the Germans came back and exhumed the bodies and transferred them by truck to another grave called "Ravin de l'Ours" near Linchamps. As news of the massacre leaked to the local townspeople, they realized the extent of the murderous intent of their occupiers.

Maj. Bollardière and Lt. Layton regrouped their men back deeper into the gorges of the Ardennes and put out 24-hour watches to alert them of German patrols. In answer to their repeated requests by radio for more guns and ammunition, OSS headquarters scheduled several more airdrops over the next several weeks. The drop team back at Tempsford had to await good weather and the next full moon. Maj. Bollardière did not intend to let the massacre of his men go unanswered; daily he put out patrols to harass the Germans and nightly they conducted sabotage missions to destroy rail lines and telephone/telegraph lines. He even left threatening letters bearing his signature for the German commanders, daring them come deeper in the mountains to attack him. The Germans knew, of course, that with no roads to convey their armored vehicles, they would be at a disadvantage in the deep crevices and ravines. Nevertheless, they sent out patrols on foot trying to locate the audacious Major who dared to threaten them.

The Ardennes Area of France

About the 29th of July 1944 one of the scout squads returned to the camp with two bedraggled men that they had picked up on their rounds. The scouts were deeply suspicious of any strangers traveling alone through the mountains, and since they claimed to be American flyers, they brought them to Lt. Layton for interrogation. The men said they had both been shot down and had managed to evade the Germans and were trying to walk to Spain; the first one said his name was Dave Talbott, and the one with the limp said his name was Cornell Shaddix.

Chapter 6

Cornell and the Resistance

When Cornell finally woke up, he tried to get up and found his knee was even more swollen than the day before. While he was sitting on the edge of the bed, the older couple came in together smiling, with the wife still talking away to her husband, all the while displaying clothes that she brought with her. She carried a faded shirt that was darned in spots, but seemed about his size. Cornell could see the worn pants, on the other hand, were clearly too short. From the amount of hand waving and gestures, Cornell understood that they wanted him to get out of his muddy flying coveralls and into less-conspicuous clothes. The older man motioned for Cornell to remove his shoes, took them and disappeared out the door, so Cornell struggled out of the coveralls and donned the pants and shirt. Just as he thought, the pants were too short. The lady came back in, saw the pants that were much too short, threw up her hands, and motioned for him to give them back. She stood there, hands on hips waiting, so Cornell removed the pants and gave them back to her, standing there clad only in his long underwear. She took the pants and left. When the man returned shortly, Cornell's brown military oxfords had been neatly blackened to appear more like civilian ones. He was waving them to dry whatever type of shoe dye he had administered. The next pair of pants was much longer, so apparently she approved.

When Cornell emerged from the back bedroom attired in civilian clothes, the older couple beamed at his new look and motioned for him to sit down to eat with them. From their small portions of potatoes and turnips it was clear that they were existing on limited rations. Talking with gestures and a smattering of English words, the couple apologized that they were not able to get a doctor or nurse for him. They explained that the German troops had seen blood around the cockpit of the crashed plane and since none of the captured crew was bloody, the Germans were keeping all local medical personnel under close surveillance in an attempt to find the wounded crewmember. Even an aspirin would have helped the pain in his leg, but the couple had no medicine.

Another immediate problem was the language barrier. Cornell recalled his first few days of trying to make sense of what they were saying:

"I was struggling to learn several hundred nouns and verbs of the Flemish language. It seemed to my modest and uninformed opinion to be about halfway between English and German but the sentence structure was impossible. It would be well to point out that Belgium is a bi-lingual country. . . Flemish is spoken in the north where they have a common border with Holland and where Flemish is virtually universal. To the south, French is the norm. This created a problem for me after I was moved south and had to start a new language all over again."

The next day another man arrived with a coat, tie, and camera. They helped Cornell put on the coat and tie, and motioned for him to sit in a straight-backed chair and stood back as the newcomer took photographs, all the while muttering "voor pasaporte." They conveyed the idea that he would need identity papers as soon as possible. When an official-looking "pasaporte" complete with some sort of seal was delivered a couple of days later Cornell was impressed with their counterfeiting ability and intrigued to find that his correct name had been used on the document. He had to assume that his name did not sound so strange in the Flemish language. The couple explained the ramifications of the information on the identity papers:

"This pasaporte did nothing for my ego however, since it stated that I was both deaf and dumb and I was instructed to groan and flap my tongue and salivate all over

anyone unknown to me who stopped me on the street. In addition, I was told that if I was queried by a German it would help matters if I would bite down hard on my tongue and expectorate a bit of blood on them . . . Anyhow the dumb portion was a natural for me. I believe my residence was listed as the local funny farm."

Cornell's "Pasaporte" picture

Two days later, Cornell was moved to another safe house where he had to struggle to get up the stairs to an upper bedroom. The next morning, Cornell heard a loud commotion downstairs and grasped that two strangers were forcing their way into the house:

"Being apprehensive, I hobbled over to the bedroom door and stood behind it while pulling the door knob tightly against myself to keep the door as close to the wall as possible. (I was much skinnier in those days). A man came into my room, made a cursory inspection of the closet, then rushed out to another part of the house after being called by

the other person.   They must have been poorly trained Gestapo underlings."

The Belgian Resistance, apparently worried that some kind of security compromise had occurred, moved Cornell again, this time to a small room in the attic of a large older home beside a busy street. His new host was an elderly lady who had another roomer, a sixteen-year-old girl who had taken some high school English. The girl was a godsend because she acted as a translator as she began to teach him some Flemish and was able to answer most of his questions. She was employed as a shopkeeper and each day when she returned from work she would have Cornell practice his new language skills and go over new vocabulary words. He never did find out if the girl was a granddaughter or relative of the widow, but Cornell sensed that the elderly lady was very protective of the young girl. By this time he was able to hobble around in the house much better. The Belgians suffered fearful deprivations, particularly in food, throughout the war. One night the widow served a rare treat for her visitors, a small roast with potatoes. She referred to the roast as some type of "flesch." As Cornell and the shop girl usually practiced language training, he asked the word for the roast. She explained that it was horsemeat. The elderly lady had a little radio and nightly they would tune in to BBC from London to find out the latest news. Of course, listening to foreign broadcasts was strictly forbidden, but in this manner they were able to catch the jubilant news about the allied landings on June 6, 1944.

There had not been a successful landing across the English Channel in over 800 years. This day saw the largest invasion fleet in history, initially involving 156,000 Allied troops from the United States, the United Kingdom, Canada, Free France and Norway. They were supported by just over 5,000 ships and landing craft and accompanied by approximately 55,000 jeeps, trucks, half-tracks, tanks, and personnel carriers. Allied aircraft flew 14,674 sorties with 127 being lost. But this was just the beginning; by the end of 11 June, 326,547 troops, 54,186 vehicles and 104,428 tons of supplies had been landed on the beaches. to support the invasion effort.

Thanks to the efforts of the OSS and the code-breakers, the Allies knew the areas of strength of the Germans, their commanders, the approximate number of troops and the areas of heavy gun emplacement. The Germans, on the other hand, knew that an invasion was imminent, but had no specific location, nor of the immensity of the operation. Rainy and overcast skies preceded the invasion and caused a postponement, but this prevented the German reconnaisance aircraft from seeing the full extent of the invasion armada. They were caught completely unaware of the landing and never fully recovered. Instead of rushing their reserve troops and armor to the landing site, the Germans held their reinforcements back thinking that the real landing would take place in the Calais area, which was nearer to the British coast.

During Cornell's initial days at this shelter, he struggled to try to pick up as much of the local language as he could. He was acutely aware that his daily survival depended upon his learning as much of the language as he could absorb. He later realized that living with a Belgian family and hourly practicing their language was the best possible way to learn a foreign language. At first their guttural outbursts were incomprehensible to him, but as the days passed and he became more accustomed to their speech patterns, the words became more and more understandable and he soon became able to follow the general topic of the conversations around the dinner table. Alone in his room he would go over the new words he learned each day and practice them aloud. Reflecting on this process later, Cornell recalled that this intensive immersion in language training was pivotal in his survival in a foreign environment.

His first attempts at communication were halting, but gradually he began to make his requests understandable to his benefactors. Naturally, one of his first questions concerned the whereabouts of his crew. Cornell was gratified to learn that they had all parachuted safely from the plane, but dismayed to learn that they had all been immediately captured and hauled off to face interrogation and shipped somewhere back east. Later he learned that all captured airmen were transported by rail to Prisoner of War camps in Eastern Germany or Poland. He felt keenly that somehow he had let his men down in some way by not being able to get them all back to England. This gnawed at him daily.

Because of the allied landing, large numbers of German troops began moving through the town. Cornell was spending the days confined to his small attic room and had been warned about being spotted through the windows. Noises outside made him extremely cautious as he surveyed the street below:

"The entire division moved through this street with me watching covertly from behind some filmy curtains. . .The entire procession took three or four hours during which time hundreds upon hundreds of horse-drawn wagons went plodding by. . . They obviously had orders to rush to the new front in Normandy and passed by day and night..."

Cornell only later came to recognize the deep roots of the Belgian Resistance movement. He was just the latest in a series of downed airmen who were helped by the Resistance, many of whom lost their lives in trying to hide and assist the American and British airmen. The movement began with the surrender of the Belgian government in the summer of 1940 after facing overwhelming German military might. It was first led by former Belgian officers and soldiers who wished to continue to resist the Germans in any way possible. Because of the harsh policies of the occupying forces, the resistance movement gained in strength as Belgian civilians began to quietly add their support. Most of the resistance was passive, by means such as work slow downs, producing faulty parts for the German industries, and listening to the underground radio. But others took more active and violent means of resistance, involving sabotage of German installations and assassinations of particularly cruel occupying soldiers. The German response to the resistance was brutal. Belgian Resistors who were captured were tortured and sent to prison camps or executed. During the occupation, over 30,000 members of the resistance were captured, with approximately 16,000 Belgians either being executed or dying while in captivity.

Resistance activity picked up rapidly with the advent of the British and American bombing raids over Europe. With the number of downed flyers increasing daily, several organized routes were developed to move the flyers out of occupied Europe and into neutral Spain, where they had a chance to get back to England. The British MI9 organization, charged with assisting resistance groups, air-dropped money and supplies to support the underground movement. The best known of these routes was the famed "Comete" route, which escorted over 700 pilots through France to the Spanish border. To accomplish this, the organizers had to forge false identity cards and arrange for food and a series of safe houses along the way to pass along the flyers. The underground routes were always in danger of being exposed, for any members of the resistance who were arrested were subject to torture to try to get them to reveal information about the process. During the time the Comete Line was in existence, 140 members were arrested and executed for helping the downed airmen.

In the earlier part of the war, escaping airmen were furnished civilian clothing and false identity papers, and put on trains to make their way across France toward the Spanish border. There they were to travel by foot over the Pyrenees to cross over into Spain. But in the latter part of the war after the Germans occupied all of France the travel became more and more dangerous. Then, as the Allied air forces began to destroy the French rail system in the build up to the invasion, travel by rail became less and less.

To lessen the chance of discovery, Cornell was moved again to another home in Izegem. Since this house was connected to a back yard surrounded by a high brick wall with shards of glass cemented on the top to discourage trespassers, he was at last able to go for short periods outside within the bricked enclosure. He was amazed how much he missed seeing the sunlight and being able to gaze up occasionally at the formations of bombers passing overhead on their way to Germany. Since the back yard was muddy, he was furnished a pair of wooden shoes with felt inserts to enable him to limp around. Wearing the shoes gave him a better understanding of the usefulness of such odd footwear.

It was in this house on the 18th of June that the partisans gave Cornell a small birthday party in honor of his 24th birthday and to encourage him to continue to work on his language skills and to keep on exercising his knee. Almost 6 weeks had passed since he had been shot down. He was deeply touched and honored by their care and vowed never to forget the sacrifices they were making to rescue downed flyers. As his knee was getting better, they furnished him a bicycle and two companions to bike around the town, all the while avoiding any passing German troops. As the resistance members saw that Cornell's strength was returning, they sent him along with the two companions back to the village of Ardooie–near the area where his plane had crashed–to be hidden at a farm home. There Cornell heard a heart-warming story:

"When my crew had been marched to the local hoosegow (some hobbling from injuries) they passed a large group of gathering citizens who suddenly broke out in loud spontaneous applause. The kraut guards began firing their weapons in the air and yelling "Raus!" German for get the hell out of here. The crowd was quickly dispersed."

Photo courtesy of John Buckel

Ol' Dad crashed in Ardooie, Belgium

Cornell observed that the latest farmhouse he was staying in was built along the lines of the Southern "Dog Trot" house, with a hallway running down the middle with both ends open to the outside. The only marked difference from the Southern ones was the fact that this home was entirely constructed of double-walled brick and looked very substantial. By this time Cornell could follow conversations in Flemish and offer an occasional reply or ask a question in their language. Over an oil lamp after the dinner meal late one night, the man of the house had an extended conversation and related to Cornell his hatred of the invaders:

"(they were)...aggressors who had been tramping over their land since the dawn of time, stealing everything in sight, raping their girls, killing the men, all kinds of crime, and they were sure were getting tired of it. Of course I was aware of a smattering of this bit of history, and my heart goes out to those gentle people and does to this day."

Upon departing this friend's home, Cornell was given a medal of the patron saint of travel, St. Christopher, in the hope they could send him some good fortune along the way. Cornell remarked later, *"My lot did not seem to improve as a result of them, but the kind thoughts were appreciated."*

Cornell was repeatedly shuffled around from home to home, mainly for security reasons, but also, he suspected, to spread the burden of another mouth to feed in times of extreme food shortage. Nothing was ever hinted about this burden, but Cornell was always careful to eat the smallest portions as he could, never wasting any food and following the eating habits of his hosts, but he was always aware of how close the people were to famine.

About 275 miles to the west, the Allies remained confined to the beaches, hemmed in with the dense hedgerows and well-placed German defenders. At first, the hedgerows virtually stopped the Allied tanks, for they forced the tank to try to climb over, which exposed their underbelly, which was lightly armored. But changes were in the air, for an American infantryman devised a clever way to destroy the hedgerows. He welded four tusk-like prongs to the front of a Sherman tank, which allowed the tank to rip a path through the hedgerows while remaining roughly level. The innovation was quickly adopted across the narrow front. The welders even used scrap metal from Rommel's underwater obstacles to provide the parts. The Allies continued to reinforce their initial landing effort, pouring in more men, ammunition, tanks, and trucks.

After staying in Ruddervoorde about a month, the partisans made arrangements for Cornell to be escorted by two Belgian bikers to Brussels. As the escorts arrived wearing short pants for this warmer day Cornell could not help but see their well-muscled legs from using the bicycle as a primary mode of transportation. Cornell was introduced to the older of the two who said he was Jose Gilles de Pelichey and the other who said he was a Belgian police officer. Cornell was instructed to ride about 100 meters behind the two and if they were stopped by any German patrols he was to turn and ride down a side road or pull over and appear to work on his bike. The two seasoned bikers set a quick pace, one quicker than Cornell could keep up with, so occasionally they would slow down to allow him to catch back up. In this manner they traveled to the much larger city of Brussels.

Cornell learned after the war that the leader of his biking companions, de Pelichey, was arrested by the Gestapo within weeks after their trip to Brussels for suspected partisan activity. Cornell was sure that de Pelichey had been deeply involved in the underground networks since the beginning of the occupation. He was subjected to a lengthy interrogation and sent to the concentration camp at Gusen-Mauthausen in Austria, where he died on 26 October 1944.

In Brussels Cornell was finally put in contact with some elements of the escape pipeline and arrangements were made to begin to shuffle him towards the French border. His host in Brussels was Madame Claire Du Vister. Her partner, an older gentleman who spoke excellent English, told Cornell that they had to be extremely careful about contacting members of the escape route, since they had been compromised in the past, and members who were helping the downed aviators had been arrested and tortured. Cornell learned after the war that Madame Du Vister *"was arrested some three weeks later and sent to Buchenwald where she survived brutal treatment and was repatriated after the war. She is reported to have helped seventeen Allied airmen, including me. God Bless her."*

When they were ready to place him in the escape pipeline, the new guide told Cornell that they would start by walking a few blocks in the open to a streetcar stop. Cornell was to follow his guide always keeping about ten meters distance. When the guide stopped to wait for a streetcar, Cornell was to wait some distance away. When the streetcar stopped, Cornell was to quickly enter and sit a few seats away from his guide.

Cornell did as he was told, and the trip was uneventful until he boarded the open-sided streetcar as instructed and sat on one of the empty double seats at the rear of the car. At the next stop, a German Oberlieutenant boarded and without giving the driver a token, walked directly to the back of the car and sat down beside Cornell. Cornell froze and did not say a word. Thankfully, neither did the German Officer. After a few blocks the German rose and ordered to driver to stop in front of a large office building. He got off. Cornell breathed easier.

Finally, the guide stood to get off at the edge of town, and Cornell followed him into a small building. There he was given a bike and wished a fond farewell. Cornell vividly remembers the next moments: "*He pointed out a beautiful young girl one hundred meters down the road to the south, and told me to follow her, maintaining this same distance, and if she stopped for any reason, I was to keep going and not to worry, the resistance would find me. With legs weakened by injury and idleness, I had a tough time keeping up with my guide, who had spent her life on a bike. She had the most distracting habit of allowing her full skirt to blow up around her waist in the wind, and of the hundred or so kraut guards we passed, not a one paid any attention to me.* "

After biking several hours to the south, the girl stopped and entered an isolated house. After a few moments, Cornell entered, but the girl had gone out the back and disappeared. He never got the chance to thank her, or even find out her name. He was introduced to his new male guide who did not wish to give his name and two new evaders, a British and an American airman, both of whom were gunners. Together they biked several hours to the village of Riviere, about eight miles south of Namur.

In Riviere Cornell and his new companions were led to a large Catholic parsonage, where they found, to Cornell's amazement, 6 British, 1 Canadian, and 22 American airmen. He learned that this was the last stop in the Underground Railroad system that sent evaders on the French railway system to the Spanish frontier.

However, the recent bombing raids (including Cornell's accurate placement of bombs) had destroyed most of the French rail system in the buildup to the D-Day invasion. What few trains running were crowded with German soldiers being rushed to the front, hence the big backlog of evaders. Cornell stayed in the parsonage from about the 15th to the 24th of July.

Here at the parsonage Cornell met a new pal and soon to be sidekick, David Russell Talbott, recently a member of the 44th Bomb Group, piloting a B-24. Cornell remembers: *"He was a pilot whose aircraft had precipitately blown up over Holland. He had awakened on the ground with Dutch civilians working over him trying to bring him back from the dead as they viewed the situation and he had a small piece of shrapnel buried deep in his upper back. Perhaps the explosion blew his chute open; he could not remember pulling the "D" ring for chute deployment. Several of his crew suffered fatalities which weighed heavily on him"*

Of course, finding enough food and preparing it worked an extreme hardship on the Belgian underground.

Cornell and Dave began to grow alarmed at the sheer number of airmen hidden away at the parsonage. They also observed the extreme chances the resistance members were taking at trying to hide such a large group of evaders all in one place.

So, after about ten days of waiting, Cornell and Dave decided to take matters into their own hands. In Cornell's words: *"Dave and I talked ourselves into the most stupid decisions of all time. We decided that the best idea would be for us to strike out on our own for the Spanish border, walking yet. I'm not sure that I was aware that this destination was six hundred miles away as the crow flies, although I knew it would be a long, tough trip."*

The other evaders attempted to talk Cornell and Dave out of the attempt. The resistance members also tried to dissuade them, but finally gave in to their wishes to travel. Their benefactors were able to at least provide them with three loaves of bread and one kilo of sugar. The pair left the parsonage and headed generally westward, always sticking to back roads. One immediate problem was that they had no map of the area. After walking all day and into the night, they slept fitfully on the ground under a large tree. On the second night the rain began to fall and they sneaked into a small barn and spent the night on a nice pile of hay. They left just before daybreak.

Meanwhile back west at Normandy, the Allies finally began to make progress moving beyond the beachhead. The original plan for the invasion drew upon the lessons learned in North Africa. There the Americans had taken advantage of their mobility to wage a fast-moving attack before the Germans had time to reinforce their lines. Eisenhower and Bradley were well aware that when two opposing armies dug in, the resulting static trench warfare was too costly in terms of men and material. They were determined to avoid the stalemate that cost so many lives during World War I. Therefore they planned to hit one particular spot in the German line with everything they had and pour all their tanks and motorized columns through the opening. Their entire attack plan was built on the concept of rapid deployment and speed.

They chose a point just beyond the town of St.-Lo to hit. Calling upon the bombers of the 8th Air Force, they targeted a "carpet" of bombs to saturate an area just in front of the Americans. Unfortunately, a few of the bombs fell short and killed some American troops, including the American General Leslie McNair. But the carpet bombing absolutely shattered the German resistance at that point. So on July 25, 1944 the Americans poured through the breach in the German lines and instead of costly yards of progress, raced for miles before the Germans had time to reorganize a defense. The Germans reeled backwards toward the Seine while the Allied Armies pushed their tanks to the limit to race across the open plains. The "breakout" at St.-Lo would be the beginning of the end of the German occupation of France. Cornell did not know it at the time, but Patton's army was racing across France toward him and the Rhine River.

Cornell remembers his first sight of the Ardennes Forest: *"After four days we were relieved to come across an enormous forest which afforded us cover and which was cut through by a huge chasm. I know now that this was the Meuse (Maas in upper Belgium) River in the Ardennes Forest, so we had to alter course to the south rather than traverse the deep canyon and swim across the river."*

Their meager supply of food exhausted, the two men continued to walk westward, gradually growing weaker and not really aware of how much danger they were in by trespassing in this area. Cornell stated: *"We were not aware of it at the time, but we were in a notoriously active Maquis territory, and wanderers found in this area were frequently shot on sight by the Germans as assumed partisans. The Maquis, on the other hand, had a poor disposition to interlopers."*

They crossed the French border sometime during the night and by daybreak arrived at the little town of Nouzonville, France. They were at the limit of their endurance so they decided to enter a Catholic Church on the outskirts of town to ask for help. David Talbott remembers their plight: *"We'd always been instructed that in situations like this, a good choice would be around a church where we could go in and wait. Cornell was too weak to walk by then so I hid him in the woods and walked back to Rivera (?), a church in the village. I'd guess it was a Catholic Church. There was a young woman there but I guess I scared her as she wasn't very friendly or receptive to me.* Approaching a sister, he uttered the words "Americains" and she froze, then flew into a panic and ran to the back of the church. Shortly thereafter, a gruff and mature man came in and began to question him.

Apparently satisfied that they were genuine evaders, and not German imposters sent to gather information, he explained that he had to be very careful. He then asked Dave to wait outside in a nearby grove of trees where Cornell was resting until dark while he notified his contacts.

Just after the sky became completely dark a group of about eight young men who were all wearing civilian clothes but sporting identical black berets approached them. They were all armed with American M-1 carbines, the same one that Cornell had carried in the swamps of Louisiana. Cornell wondered how on earth they came to be in possession of the carbines. Later he found out about the supply air drops. Motioning for Cornell and Dave to follow them, they started in a single file deeper into the forest. All this time they were very quiet and refused to talk: *"One man led the way (it turned out he was one of the Maquis Lieutenants) while the others walked behind us, and the one thing certain was that we were being closely watched. This was truly a tough bunch, as was emphatically demonstrated later."* With his injured leg, Cornell struggled to keep up with their fast pace across the rugged terrain.

Chapter 7

Prisoners of War

The exact geography of the crash site of "Ol Dad" was crucial to the events that swiftly followed. First, since the aircraft had made it back almost to the coast of Belgium, the crew was far from irate German civilians who had a propensity to harm the flyers who had bombed them night and day. But at the same time, their crash scene near the village of Ardooie, Belgium as Cornell later learned, was only a short distance from a German outpost. They came down so close to the garrison that some of the crewmembers, who all opened their parachutes quickly, were actually fired upon by German troops while still descending.

In recalling this moment, Cornell stated: *"We had been briefed repeatedly that delaying the chute opening would enhance the probability of escape from the bad guys. As I left the plane, I got a glimpse of my crew's opened chutes. I do not fault my guys for the early chute deployment since jumping out of an aircraft in flight is a rather hairy experience."*

The crew really had no opportunity to escape. Although the German soldiers were quick to apprehend all the crewmembers as each one landed, they were under strict orders to detain and transport any downed airmen to a Gestapo field outfit who handled all interrogations in the occupied territories. Their intelligence unit roughly interrogated each crewmember separately as they arrived. The Gestapo was very familiar with the makeup of a typical B-17 crew and soon established that one pilot was missing. A visit by the Gestapo to the remains of the crashed plane revealed some traces of blood in the cockpit, which came from a minor wound at Cornell's wrist. For this reason the German authorities sent out search teams looking for a wounded flyer in the local area. However, by this time Cornell had been spirited away by the resistance and his parachute located and the cloth cut up and made into other garments.

Tail Gunner Hugh Hamilton recalls that fateful day:" *I was shot down on April 27, '44 – less than two weeks before D-Day. Everyone knew the invasion was imminent – didn't know which day, though. The Germans were ready. They were gathered all along the French-*

Belgian coast. We were making short flights across the English Channel, attacking the German installations.

On my "Big Day", we made our usual short flight, landed home safely, and then we're told we were to make another raid – No. 13. Something told me this was it. Anyway, we loaded up again, hit our target somewhere down in France and headed back – probably 100 bombers or more in our formation. Nearing the channel, a lone battery of anti-aircraft guns fired at us. The five burst of flak blew our plane out of formation – no other plane was touched. The flak cut our fuel lines, and killed 3 of our 4 engines, but luckily, no one was hit.

The plane struggled along on one engine, losing altitude, of course. We threw out flak vests and everything we could to lighten the load. Finally, a few minutes later, fire broke out in the one engine. Shad, the pilot, said, "That's it, boys. Get out!"

I snapped my chute in place and went up into the body of the plane. I'd promised the ball gunner that if this ever happened, I'd be sure he got out of the turret, but he was already out of the plane. The others were either out, or ready to jump. As I went out the door, I had the thought – make a delayed jump – don't pull the ripcord too soon – they won't see you as long. Yet, out of the plane, I counted to 7, said "this isn't enough" – pulled the ripcord anyway. I waited to see the chute open, but nothing happened. The ripcord – a chrome hand-sized loop attached to a wire that holds the chute together – was still in my hand. I looked at it, ran my left hand down the wire – totally disengaged.

So I stuffed the ripcord into my pocket – don't ask why – and pulled the flap on the chute; then the chute opened and blossomed above me. Hanging there, swinging around, I looked around for the first time. Saw two other chutes in the distance – lower.

It didn't take too long to hit the ground. Three thumps – feet, rear end, then the back of my head. Sitting up, I saw the chute collapse in front of me. Unhooking it, I stood up, brushing Brussels sprouts off. I'd landed in a woman's garden.

Several civilians ran toward me, smiling and talking, but I didn't understand them. Women hugged me and kids shook my hand. Probably thought I was starting D-Day. I tried to get away – they were showing the Germans where I was. A woman caught my hand and pulled me into her house and into her basement. Hearing thumping upstairs, I went through the basement window and across the yard. Another woman pulled me into her kitchen and gave me a glass of milk.

As I gulped it down, two Germans came in the door with guns leveled at me. I drained the glass, sat it down, and raised my arms." The crewmembers were taken first to a prison near Brussels where they were detained about 10 days and initially interrogated. Then the German soldiers separated the captured officers, Copilot 2nd Lt. George Sullivan and Bombardier 2nd Lt. Cole Dailey from the rest of the enlisted men and put them with some other British officers who had been recently captured. The officers were then transported out of Belgium by rail all the way across Germany to a prisoner-of-war camp about

100 miles southeast of Berlin in the province of Lower Silesia. There a Prisoner of War (POW) Camp near the town of Sagan had been established in 1942 for captured airmen who were of officer rank. When the men arrived they learned the name of their destination was Stalag Luft III. The site had been chosen for its loose, sandy soil, which would make tunneling very difficult.

Sullivan, Dailey, and the other new British arrivals found the camp to be on a high state of alert with a newly installed Camp Commandant and severe rules with drastic punishment for the slightest infraction. They soon learned that about a month prior to their arrival, the POW camp had experienced a major escape on the night of 24 March 1944. Although several attempts had been made earlier, this one entailed a massive excavation of deep tunnels from underneath a prisoner hut to just outside the main fence. The tunnels were marvels of engineering, reinforced with boards taken from prisoner beds, a continuous air supply, and interior electric lighting. At the same time, the prisoners who planned to attempt to escape were preparing forged identity papers, civilian clothing, and railway timetables and maps. A total of 76 men were selected to escape through the tunnel during the night.

The Hollywood film, "*The Great Escape*" was a fictionalized version of their attempt, and although some American prisoners worked on the tunnel, all of the escapees were British, Norwegian, or Dutch airmen. Unfortunately, only three escapees finally made it to freedom; all the rest were soon caught with fifty being executed and the others sent back to Stalag Luft III or transferred to other POW camps. The presiding Commandant was sacked and the Gestapo shot some German workers who had not reported the thefts of materials.

The diet supplied to the prisoners was inadequate, but it was partially supplemented by food parcels from the American, British, and Canadian Red Cross. The food parcels were not delivered individually, but combined and distributed to the POWs equally. The camp was first opened in 1942, but as more and more prisoners arrived, it was enlarged in 1943 and again in 1944. Most of the POWs arriving in 1944 were, like Cornell's crew, American airmen. The compound consisted mostly of single story huts about 10 by 12 feet containing 5 triple bunk beds. Eventually the entire camp enclosed about 60 acres surrounded by tall barbed wire fences and lighted guard towers that overlooked the huts and exercise yard.

Promptly upon arrival, Sullivan and Dailey were searched, fingerprinted, photographed, and given a cursory examination by the German Camp authorities. The International Red Cross was notified of their presence. Since the Red Cross routinely passed along this notification to the Air Force, they assumed that their next-of-kin would be notified. The Americans were separated from the British flyers in their group and delivered to the American portion of the compound. There the new arrivals were greeted by an Air Force Colonel who identified himself as the senior officer at the section where they would be confined. He told Sullivan and Daily that the prisoners had been allowed to organize their part of the prison camp along lines similar to the U.S. Army. He explained that the senior POWs had found that through organization, they lived better, ate better, and got along better under the trying conditions of a P.O.W. camp. He impressed upon them the necessity of learning the camp rules quickly, obeying them, and trying to get along with their fellow prisoners. He then stated that for the next few days, they would be segregated from the other prisoners until their backgrounds could be checked out.   He explained that this procedure was necessary because the Germans, wishing to know the innermost details of the camp prisoners, had on occasion tried to slip an English speaking imposter into the camp to gain information about escape attempts or prison contraband such as radios or saws.

The next day, Sullivan and Dailey were interrogated separately by American Intelligence POWs about their home background, Air Force training, previous assignments, and past missions.   Only after the officials were satisfied that both men were who they claimed to be did they enter the regular camp life. Just like in basic training, the camp operated according to definite rules of sleeping, eating, exercising, and cleaning. They learned that the meager German food supplies, mostly bread and potatoes, was supplemented by the Red Cross parcels, and that each hut organized and prepared their own food, trying to divide the inadequate supplies as fairly as possible among all the prisoners. Even with the addition of supplies from the Red Cross, their daily nutrition was inadequate, so all the men steadily lost weight as they existed on the sparse offerings. One of the most important components of the Red Cross parcels was cigarettes, which the men could use to bribe the weaker of the German guards for batteries or supplies. They also bribed some guards to get advance notice of inspections, so they could hide a banned radio. They were astounded to learn that the prisoners had obtained a working radio so they could keep up with the news of the war being broadcast by the BBC. Each night, a member of the intelligence staff would appear and give a short briefing on the war situation. The new arrivals were warned never to speak of what they learned in these nightly briefings or their whole hut would be skipped over for four days. This was done to enforce security.

Both Sullivan and Dailey were impressed by the extent of the complexity of the organization within the camp. They were assigned to blocks, with each block containing about one hundred men, and further subdivided into combines, with each combine containing twelve men each. They would eat, sleep, and work with their combine, which became literally their new family.

The prisoners had managed, mostly through the Red Cross, to accumulate a large library and the prisoners were allowed to visit and check out the books. Even with the inadequate diet, the prisoners were encouraged to take daily walks and to try to keep active and healthy. On Sundays virtually all attended one of the many church services throughout the day. Card games, again, with cards supplied by the Red Cross, helped to pass the time.

Most prisoners ended up sleeping about 12 hours a day, which helped conserve their strength.

One of the most important events, at least to the Germans, was roll call. This was taken twice a day at set times in the morning and in the evening. The guards took this procedure very seriously. Each and every prisoner was individually counted and duly recorded. The men were confined to their barracks at 9:00 p.m.

Near the end of the war in January 1945, Soviet troops had advanced to within 16 miles of the camp, so the prisoners, totaling at this time about 11,000, were marched westward through deep snow to other camps. They were liberated by units of the U.S. 14th Armored Division on 29 April 1945. Along with all the other POWs, Sullivan and Dailey were evacuated to field hospitals in France, where they went through a de-lousing procedure, were issued new clothes, then underwent a complete medical checkup. At the same time, they were being fed a calorie-laden diet designed to build up their strength. On their fifth day there, they were interviewed by the Records section and Intelligence agents. They filled out dozens of forms and answered hundreds of questions from Intelligence about their bailout, their capture, and their camp experiences. Both Sullivan and Dailey persisted in trying to find out what happened to the rest of their crew, and were relieved to find out that most of them had survived. From the Army Field hospital, they were loaded on a boat to return to America.

The rest of Cornell's enlisted crew, including Sergeants Erb, Hale, Cornelius, Hamilton, Lee, Cortelletty, and Lestico, were first sent to the same prison near Brussels where they were confined in individual cells and interrogated.   After about 10 days they were separated from the officers and all the enlisted men were sent by rail along the Rhine River to Frankfort, when each member was further interrogated.   There their identification was delivered to the International Red Cross as prisoners of war.

One topic that is sure to bring controversy is the exact nature of the role the International Red Cross played in bringing relief to the Allied POW camps in Germany and adjacent countries during World War II. Of the 200,000 Americans who served in the 8th Air Force in Britain, slightly over 28,000 became prisoners of war after their planes were shot down over Germany or territories controlled by Germany. All the countries that signed the Geneva Convention in 1929, including Germany, agreed to allow qualified relief agencies to visit and monitor the camps, to exchange identification information, and to distribute goods to the prisoners.   Although the practice was followed in general, numerous instances of violations of the Geneva Convention occurred. In the majority of cases, Germany allowed the Red Cross, which was headquartered in Geneva, Switzerland, to make periodic visits to POW camps (but not their concentration camps) to deliver food and parcels to prisoners, and to make records of identification for purposes of notifying prisoners' families.

There is no doubt that some food and parcels, maybe a majority, sent to the prisoners disappeared on the way or were never delivered. But in many cases the Red Cross food and clothing saved lives. In 1944 the International Red Cross was awarded the Nobel Peace Prize for its efforts to aid prisoners and refugees. Although the Red Cross was more successful in bringing some aid to Allied POW camps, the organization was unable to bring relief to the many concentration camps in German held territory because of the fanatical opposition of the Nazi leaders. In the end, the Red Cross dropped its efforts to bring assistance to the concentration camps in order not to damage its efforts to aid the Allied POWs. This failure to bring help to the victims of concentration camps has been considered by some the greatest failure of the International Committee of the Red Cross.

The enlisted men of Cornell's crewmembers were then loaded into boxcars and transported to a newly constructed POW camp near what is now Gross Tychow, Poland. The name of their new residence was Stalag Luft IV. Opened in May of 1944, the POW camp would eventually house just over 8,000 American airmen and almost 1,000 British, Polish and Czech airmen. The camp consisted of five compounds separated by barbed wire fences with the POWs housed in about 40 wooden barracks. About 200 men were assigned to each barrack. They were all unheated with no bathing facilities and only open-air latrines were provided. In October 1944 the International Red Cross described conditions in the POW camp as bad and getting worse. The prisoners had no way of washing up so they were plagued by fleas and lice.

160 FALLEN FORTRESS

What clothing they were issued was in poor condition and no undergarments were provided.

Each compound had its own kitchen, which was used to prepare the food, mostly potatoes and bread, furnished by the Germans. Parcels of food from the International Red Cross supplemented this, but the delivery was sporadic. Consequently, many times the prisoners had to go on half rations until the next parcels arrived. In a similar manner, their clothing supplies, which was furnished by the Red Cross, was inadequate, especially for the coming winter of 1944. For medical attention, there were three American doctors and one British, along with one British dentist. The small infirmary had about 132 beds, but the doctors were confined to their huts at night when no medical help was available. Their mail arrived irregularly but was sent out about once a week.

A significant part of the problem lay in the huge numbers of prisoners of war. Germany, under increasing pressure from the Soviet armies in the east and the Allied armies in the west, and under round-the-clock bombardment from the skies, was not adequately prepared to provide food and shelter for the thousands of prisoners that resulted from the air war.

In February 1945 as the Soviet armies began to approach from the east, German authorities ordered the prisoners, who were already suffering from malnutrition and disease, to set out on a march to the west that was later to be called "The Black March." Cornell's tail gunner, Hugh Hamilton, later described the experience:

"Anyway, on Feb. 6, '45, about 10,000 of us POWs were evacuated from Stalag IV, Russians approaching again. We were put into groups of 100 to 200, with a few old Germans for guards, and headed west. We stayed on back roads, leaving main roads for military use.

When available, we would take over a farm and sleep in the barn. Any food we could find was eaten. If no barn was handy, we slept under bushes, in a field; wherever. Fortunately, I'd acquired a big British overcoat, so I'd wrap it around me; draw up my feet and sleep.

Food was always a problem. As spring came, I got dysentery for several weeks. As the days went by, I decided if nothing is put in, nothing can come out. So for 3 days I ate nothing, but had to run anyway. So much for my logic!"

Lasting a total of 86 days, the prisoners were forced to march in the snow and the rain with inadequate provisions or shelter. They drank water from ditches on the side of the road or ate snow. The stronger prisoners assisted the weaker ones. Some of those who could not maintain the pace were either shot or bayoneted. Many times they were forced to backtrack where they had just been to avoid the encroaching Allied armies. Finally in May 1945 the prisoners were located along the banks of the River Elbe near Lauenberg, Germany when they were liberated by elements of the British Army.

Every member of Cornell's crew survived the ordeal of being a prisoner of war and was repatriated back to the United States.

Chapter 8

Cornell, Victor, and the Maquis

After walking all night through the rough mountainous region, just before daylight the leader of the Maquis stopped and made a whistling, chirping sound as Cornell was just about at the end of his endurance. The same sound came lilting back from a nearby hill so the men continued up the forested hillside to a small clearing on a gentle mound. As Cornell limped into the clearing, he saw it contained a group of about forty to fifty men who were gathered around a central fire that looked like it was set up for cooking, ringed with parachutes rigged as tents. Like the squad that had brought him and Dave in, all the men were dressed in different kinds of outfits but everyone was wearing the customary black beret with the round emblem on the front. Two of the men were dressed in military uniforms. The younger looking of the two, wearing the silver bar of a 1st lieutenant, held a rapid conversation in French briefly with Cornell's escorts and then walked over and extended his hand to Dave and Cornell. "My men tell me you fellows are pilots trying to walk to Spain," he said in slightly accented English. "How in the world did you ever end up here in the middle of the Ardennes?" he asked, and then introduced himself as "Victor."

Cornell and Dave poured out their individual stories of how they had both survived a bailout of a crippled plane that was going down and been assisted by the friendly Belgian and Dutch people. Victor stopped them several times to ask penetrating questions about the church they had stayed, the names of their helpers, and details of their travels. Then he led the pair to talk of their pilot training, the bases where they had been assigned and life at the British aerodromes. Although he was extremely cordial, Cornell realized he was gently interrogating them to make sure they were not German imposters sent to gather information. Finally he seemed to be satisfied with their stories, so he held a quick conversation in French with the older man, a major in the uniform of the Free French army.

Only then were Cornell and Dave fed a very frugal meal consisting of a slice of bread and soup that Cornell learned later was lentils, and allowed to rest for the remainder of the day and to regain their strength. That evening, feeling much better after a day of resting and eating, Cornell and Dave spent half the night talking with Victor filling them in about the current situation of the war. He drew a rough map of the progress of the Allied armies and mentioned that Gen. Patton's 3rd Army was leading the way in their sector. He gave some details of the recent massacre of their green troops and what he knew of the progress of the Allies after the invasion. He then gave them a summary of his own background and how he came to serve with the OSS. His command of native German was superb:

"A smooth talker and apparently fearless, he once stopped along a road and helped two German soldiers repair a bicycle flat tire. He established rapport with them, posing as a minor kraut official which his phony passport bore out. He came back with an incredible amount of information, which was promptly relayed over our little radio to London. . . .He was an exceptionally brave person and I salute his memory."

Cornell realized when Victor gave them the story of his own unique background and how he came to be fighting with the Maquis that he did indeed trust the two airmen. That first day Cornell saw that life in the camp was organized in a very military manner with guards being posted in a round-the-clock watch. All day long the Major sent out teams of four to six men similar to the one that found him and Dave to reconnoiter the surrounding mountains. At sunup and sundown the flag was raised and lowered in a military ceremony. Early the next morning was when the radio was activated, for this was the best time for transmission and reception. The radio operator Brault obtained Cornell and Dave's identification and prepared a coded message that was sent back to OSS headquarters notifying them of their presence with the Maquis.   Cornell later learned that this message was passed along to his grateful parents, who had not heard a word since the initial missing in action telegram and had no idea if he was dead or alive. The Maquis also gave a daily radio report on the Germans they had spotted, along with their unit identification and numbers. Cornell and Dave learned that over 120 of these OSS teams were spread out across France daily relaying information concerning German troop numbers and units. It was also during this same radio code exchange that they learned that their esteemed commander, Maj. Bolidierre, had been promoted by the Free French to Lt. Colonel. They of course had no insignia to pin on him, but Cornell noted that the entire camp switched immediately to referring to him as "Col. Prism." The commandant's left arm had clearly been injured in the past and he carried it constantly across his stomach.   Cornell and Dave were told of his extensive military background and that he had not only served with the French Foreign Legion but also in North Africa and in the Italian campaign. His favorite weapon was a German P-38 semi-automatic sidearm, using of course ammunition taken from dead soldiers. Each night the flag was lowered in a moving ceremony that brought some of the Frenchmen to tears. Their country had been forcefully invaded and each one felt he had to uphold the honor of their compatriots. At the same time, they were reminded daily that capture by the Germans meant certain death and for this reason they took no prisoners. The camp cook was a quite elderly man who prepared their food under very difficult conditions. The newcomers thought he accomplished wonders with almost no equipment. Cornell learned more details of the cook's background:

"The story was that he had lost two sons to Hun firing squads, presumably due to partisan activity with the maquis. This old fellow cursed 'Le Boche' with every other breath. Captured German guards were routinely brought into camp and he did the honors. 'Pour Henri, pour Francois.' He earned his reputation as executioner."

The group moved frequently, especially after they had scheduled an airdrop or when German patrols were spotted. They took down the tents, filled in the latrine holes and tried to leave little evidence of their campsite. Cornell's job in the moving process was not complicated:

"My primary activity on our frequent moving days was to carry a very large sack of lentils, a small form of peas. To this day I love lentils. It did nothing for my ego to know that I could have been replaced by a jackass. . . I was given a rusty French bolt-action rifle made in 1870 during the Franco/Prussian war but with no ammo and no bayonet. I was wondering if I was supposed to scare Le Boche to death with it."

On the third morning after their arrival, a messenger ran into the camp and breathlessly announced that he had spotted a number of German soldiers heading their way:

"The camp became a beehive of activity, and just minutes later all hell broke loose, literally.   We had two machine guns mounted on the trail that logically had to be taken by the krauts to approach us in this rough territory. We also had two bazookas in case of the appearance of armored vehicles, but none showed, probably because the Wehrmacht could not spare them."

A burst of machine gun fire announced the arrival of the Germans, and since Cornell nor Dave had not been issued any ammunition, they retreated to the top of the hill, where Col. Bolidierre, Victor, and the radio operator had established a command post. Victor translated the commander's smiling order to the two airmen as "Take cover." Cornell and Dave jumped into a deep trench that cut through the top of the mound. The Commandant refused to take cover, but continued to stroll about the hilltop issuing orders to his troops while bullets whizzed about his head.

Cornell witnessed one young trooper who had been hit in the wrist grimacing while the company doctor worked to stop the blood loss and sew up the torn flesh. This was done without any morphine or painkillers. It was at this point that a ricochet bullet or a fragment of one struck a glancing blow across Cornell's nose and right cheek. It was hardly more than a scratch, but it gave him a momentary fright.

At this time, the Commandant recognized that the Germans, who had the Maquis badly outnumbered, began the same tactic of trying to flank both sides of the group at the same time. This time he was ready, instructing his men to retreat silently in a single column down the hillside and away from the battle. They quickly left the area undetected and trooped to a nearby mountain top where they heard sounds of firing continue for almost a full hour. They were puzzled but the Commandant grinned, as he understood that both of the German flanking movements had been firing on each other. Cornell had never seen such a smile on the Commandant's face as when he saw that the Maquis understood what had just taken place.

The Commandant then anticipated that the Germans, once they had discovered their deadly mistake, would return to their Garrison along the same road that they had entered. So he carefully placed his troops in hiding along the road to intercept and ambush the column. When the German trucks approached, it was clear that French civilians had been placed in the cab of each truck, so the order to attack was never given. The eight trucks passed so close to the Maquis that Cornell could not understand why they were not spotted. Cornell and the group were informed later that fifty-four of the Germans were killed in the action, with the loss of two Maquis. Cornell's admiration for the Commandant grew with every action.

In addition to the early time slot to transmit coded messages, Victor and the Commandant carefully listened daily to the British Broadcasting Corporation for special coded words imbedded within the broadcast requesting information or giving further instructions to the resistance groups. The timely exchange of information with the groups behind the German lines made the difference between life and death. Cornell learned that many of the members of his group had previously been smugglers during peacetime. Due to the unequal taxes on certain goods in neighboring countries, it was often profitable to hand-carry small items such as tobacco, perfumes, jewelry, and alcoholic beverages across borders for exchange. This constant traffic using the backcountry trails gave the smugglers a unique blend of skill sets that were useful during the war for the resistance groups. Cornell, raised in the hills of Winston County, Alabama where illegal whiskey manufacturing was a way of survival for many of its citizens, felt a kinship to the smugglers.

As the month of August drew to an end, the advancing Allied armies forced their way across France, causing the retreating German Divisions to move closer to the Maquis group that was sheltering Cornell and Dave. They had to stay on the move constantly. No longer could they depend on their air drops, for they shifted their location so often. For this reason, the Commandant and Victor made the decision to place Cornell and Dave at the home of a sympathizer they knew who lived near the Meuse River. Since the Germans often posted guards near the river, Cornell and Dave had to be very careful never to be seen through a window.

Sixty years later, Cornell recalled the bravery of the French families who helped the Maquis: *"Of course the local populace was subjected to intense investigation by the Gestapo after this action but since the Maquis was more active all over the place and the Krauts were sustaining heavy losses everywhere, they did not have the manpower to spare for a thorough harassment of our people. However, one group of ten suspected partisan helpers was rounded up and grilled mercilessly. Most of them were severely beaten but not one of them broke down and informed on all of us. One Belgian was given a truly severe thrashing and was admired by the rest for his steadfast courage.*

Finally, a Kraut official told the inquisitors to turn them all loose, that they represented no threat to the Germans. Five of these heroes were part of our team that helped recover supplies during air drops, and who had sons in our outfit, and two were bakers who provided us with all the bread that they could beg, borrow and steal flour for. I fervently hope they all had a good life."

After the breakout at St.-Lo, the American Armies were on firmer ground where their tanks could race ahead and their supply trucks could follow. Both Eisenhower and Bradley were in agreement to continue their breathtaking pace and race for the German border. This meant bypassing Paris with its four and one-half million population. To stop to liberate the city would mean weeks of fighting and would seriously impede their supply chain, if not crippling it for weeks.

But events in Paris caused them to reconsider. The Parisians, sick of four years of German Occupation and seeing the Allied landings on their coast, began to rise up on their own and attack the troops occupying their city. Sporadic street fighting between the partisans and the German patrols threatened to lead into wholesale slaughter of the outgunned French Resistance.

Meanwhile, Gen. de Gaulle, the head of the Free French
Army, was fearful of the role that the French Communist
Party, who had actively resisted the German Occupiers,
would play in governing post-war France. The
Communists were leading the attacks against the German
occupiers and planned to "welcome" the Allied Armies into
Paris. Gen. de Gaulle knew that if the Communist Party
were able to take partial credit for the liberation of Paris,
they would be difficult if not impossible to oust after the
war. He was determined to play the leading role in
liberating Paris, take credit for the liberation and set up
his own ruling structure.

Seeing the unfolding drama, Eisenhower and
Bradley allowed the French 2nd Armored Division, sporting
their American-supplied Sherman tanks, to lead the way
into Paris. But fearful that they were taking too long,
Bradley ordered the 4th Division to speed them along. It
worked and on August 24, a squadron of light tanks and a
company of French infantry entered the city. Gen. de
Gaulle insisted on setting up a triumphal parade for the
liberated citizens, with himself in the lead. He also
spurned the advances of the Communist partisans and
ignored their plans to be part of the post-war government.

On 3 September 1944 Cornell heard a familiar
sound of a powerful tank engine just over the hilltop
bordering the river. He and Dave excitedly climbed to the
top of the hill to be greeted by the most wonderful sight he
had seen in months, a beautiful Sherman tank with the
commander directing from the open turret. Cornell ran up
to the tank waving his arms and the Tank Commander,

surprised to see this tall peasant in ragged clothes speaking perfectly good Southern English, referred him to a nearby Captain. This was when Cornell learned he had met members of the 22nd Infantry Regiment, 4th Infantry Division, of George Patton's 3rd Army.

Cornell and Dave spent two days with the Infantry, eating their fill of Army rations and borrowing a new supply of Army uniforms to replace their ragged civilian clothes. Cornell was especially grateful for the Army boots and a real cup of coffee. They eagerly plied their benefactors for details of the invasion and subsequent break-out. They learned that the efforts of the Air Force to drive the German planes from the sky over France were largely successful. Cornell was proud to hear of the complete destruction of the French railroad marshalling yards by the 8th Air Force.

As successful evaders, Cornell and Dave were scheduled to be interviewed by the Intelligence Section back at Headquarters. Finally an empty jeep was found that could transport them back first to Laon, where they were bivouacked on a cathedral lawn. From there they were directed to Intelligence Headquarters in Paris, which had just been set up in the newly liberated metropolis only days before at the end of August.

In a stunning turn of events Paris was spared the destruction that Hitler had planned for the city. The latest commander in charge of the occupation of Paris, Gen. Dietrich von Choltitz, had been ordered to defend the city at all costs, including the lives of all his troops. Previously von Choltitz had been a loyal officer and gained a reputation for strictly following orders. But when he was summoned to Berlin to receive his instructions, he was shocked at Hitler's condition and the destruction of Berlin. He concluded that the war was probably lost.

Von Choltitz was ordered to place explosive charges on the forty-five bridges over the Seine, the French Parliament building, the power plants, and water systems in the city. Charges were also placed at the foot of the Eiffel Tower and other landmarks. Hitler knew that the city of Paris was instrumental in the battle for France. If he could not control the city, he was determined to leave a smoking ruin for the Allies to occupy. From his headquarters in Berlin Hitler had his top commander repeatedly telephone von Choltitz with the question "Is Paris burning?"

However, von Choltitz could not bring himself to destroy the beautiful city even though he had been selected as a "loyal" officer to strictly follow orders. Because the Allied Air Force controlled the skies over France, the Panzer Division that had been promised von Choltitz never arrived. When faced with the rapidly moving Allied armies, at the very last minute he surrendered the city and his troops. The explosive charges were never set off. After a period of interrogation in a British POW camp, von Choltitz spent the rest of the war in an American POW camp in Clinton, MS. After the war he returned to Germany, where he was the main source for the book, *"Is Paris Burning?"*

When an enraged Hitler learned that Paris had not been destroyed by its occupying army, he then turned to the V-missile launching sites located in Pas-de-Calais and northern France and ordered them to turn their missiles on Paris and "rain" all their might on the city. He had his aides to order the commander of the missile facilities, General Hans Speidel, to launch an attack on Paris "with all the forces at his disposal." Speidel ignored the order and was shortly thereafter arrested by the Gestapo. He spent the rest of the war in a German prison. The improbable turn of events spared the city of Paris from devastation.

As the victorious Allies swept into the city they were greeted by an incredible outpouring of celebration by the citizens who had suffered four long years under the German Occupation. To one of the first, War Correspondent Ernie Pyle, the outpouring of joy by the Parisians was "the loveliest, brightest story of our time." One visitor checked into the citadel of luxury, the Hotel Ritz. The assistant manager recognized the visitor from his prewar visits and asked the newcomer if he could offer anything as a welcoming gesture. "How about seventy-three martinis for my men?" asked Ernest Hemingway. It was a clean well-lighted hotel. The city was a study of contrasts. While the Parisians welcomed the Allied armies, bitter street fighting still continued in some areas as pockets of German resistance held out to the bitter end.

Cornell and Dave were billeted in another large ornate hotel near Notre Dame Cathedral. Cornell observed burned out German tanks still littering the streets and often heard scattered gunfire from some pockets of German soldiers who were still holed up in parts of the city. The German troops feared being captured by members of the Resistance, for the bitter partisans were known to kill their prisoners. So they hid and waited for the appearance of the Americans so they could surrender to them. Here Cornell saw one sight he would never forget:

"Now, I will swear this is the truth. I saw one French farmer coming down the way, sitting on the seat of a two-wheeled farm donkey cart and he had a German sergeant pulling the thing. He stopped near us to give his sweaty and winded beast of burden a short rest. He stuck up a conversation with us and stated that his jackass had been misappropriated by Le Boche and he had replaced it with a slower and make-do substitute."

Although many of the windows in the buildings had been shot out, Cornell observed that most of the restaurants and sidewalk cafes were open for business. People were walking in the streets, greeting the Allied troops, and offering them fruit and wine. All the radio stations continually played the French National Anthem, *La Marseilles*, with only short breaks for news from the fighting front. All the shops played their radios at full volume and the sounds filled the streets from the broken windows. Cornell vividly remembers that first day in Paris:

"Somehow I had managed to hold on to my escape kit's two thousand francs all this time and I asked a waiter if they were genuine. He took one look and said, "Oui." I asked how many liters of Champaign they would buy and he indicated eight, whereupon I told him to get them out here. Dave, and a few of our evader friends and I got

roaring drunk, and this from a fellow that seldom drinks. So, I had a lapse."

Both Cornell and Dave had to endure a lengthy debriefing from the Intelligence Division in Paris. The interviewers especially wanted to know details about how they managed to escape the Germans, who helped them to evade, and if they had personally killed any Germans. During the interrogation, Cornell unthinkingly let slip the name of one of his first benefactors at Izegem, and immediately became alarmed at divulging his name. After this slip, he did not offer any more names, fearing for their safety.

They were issued brand new uniforms and placed aboard a C-47 for a flight back to England. Cornell noted that he still had one bottle of Champaign left. No sooner had they arrived in London than they heard a horrendous explosion, which turned out to be one of the first V-2 rockets to hit the London area.

But Cornell and Dave were not the only ones arriving in London in September of 1944. The American Bandleader Glenn Miller had brought his large band over just after D-day and was staying in nearby Bedford, England. Like many other patriotic Americans, Miller wanted to join the war effort and felt his music would be an inspiration to the fighting soldiers. As a civilian he had been earning an estimated $15,000 to $20,000 per week, but he wanted to serve his country in some official capacity. Even though he was 38 years old in 1942, he persuaded the Army to let him join so that he could organize a "modernized Army band." He was commissioned as a Captain and first assigned to the Army. He was transferred to the Army Air Force and was initially assigned to Maxwell Field in Montgomery, Alabama. There Miller formed his large 50 piece Army Air Force Band and took it to England in the summer of 1944 where he and his band gave 800 performances. While in England Miller made a series of recordings at EMI's Abbey Road Studios in London that were played over Armed Forces Radio. On 15 December 1944 Miller was scheduled to fly on a single engine C-64 Norseman from England to Paris to play for the soldiers there. His plane disappeared over the English Channel and no trace was ever found of the airplane or passengers.

As soon as they arrived in London, Dave was sent to a military hospital to have the shrapnel in his back looked after, and Cornell was shipped back to the 100th Bomb Group. He did not see Dave again before the war ended.

COVER OF CORNELL'S INTERROGATION REPORT

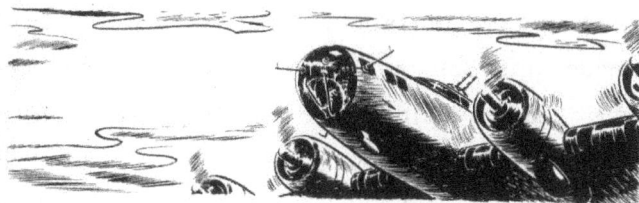

Chapter 9

Complications of the Geneva Convention

After arriving back at Thorpe-Abbotts and the "Bloody 100th", Cornell found that none of his previous roommates in his Nissen Hut were around. All had been shot down, except his old navigator, Harry Tennenbaum, who had been promoted to Captain in Cornell's absence. After Cornell's plane had been shot down, Tennenbaum was assigned to another crew and he finished out his tour.

Cornell found out his gear and personal belongings had been shipped home, never to be seen again. So he spent some of his back pay on new uniforms and personal items. When he pressed his commanders to be put back on flying regular missions, he learned of the complicated rules of the Geneva Convention: *"It seems that the U.S., being signatory to the Geneva Convention Pact after WWI, had agreed to all the conditions therein. One of the caveats allowed that if a military person entered enemy territory and evaded capture to return to friendly territory, and then returned to enemy territory, he would be subject to execution as a spy."*

The original impetus for the Geneva Convention was provided in 1859 by a Swiss citizen who had been horrified by the conditions of the wounded soldiers during wartime. This led him to try to organize a volunteer relief society to take care of the wounded during times of war. He also called for an international agreement between European countries to protect the wounded and those who cared for them. This was how the Red Cross began.

Governments were invited to send representatives to Geneva, Switzerland to an international convention to consider these issues. As a result, 12 European nations agreed in 1864 on a set of rules governing sick and wounded military personnel, regardless of nationality. They also agreed to recognize a red cross or a red crescent on a white background as a symbol of neutrality for medical personnel and hospitals. The second convention agreed to extend the protections to the armed forces at sea, and the third convention covered rules and protections for prisoners of war. Prisoners of war were to be treated humanely and not required to furnish information, except name, rank, and serial number. Germany (in particular countries that later became Germany) was a signatory to the Geneva Conventions, but later Hitler renounced the agreement. The United States tried to follow the rules of the Geneva Convention in its treatment of captured and wounded soldiers, and urged all the combatants to do likewise. Because of this, Cornell's commanders refused to allow him to go on any more missions over enemy territory, since he would be treated as a spy (and shot) if he were captured. Instead, he learned that he was slated to be returned to the States for another assignment.

Shortly afterward, along with fifty-four other evaders, he was shipped back to the United States by C-54 via Iceland, landing at LaGuardia Airport in New York, where Cornell promptly kneeled and kissed the pavement. Unfortunately, the FBI, who was worried about German infiltrators, quarantined all of the evaders for a week in a Brooklyn hotel. During the week all the evaders had to undergo lengthy questioning to prove they were indeed American soldiers. Finally satisfied, the FBI released all of them to return to their regular assignments.

After the week's delay, Cornell took another long, slow train ride south, visiting his family in Alabama on his way to his "R&R" in Miami, Florida. A hotel on the beach had been reserved for the returning warriors. But Cornell was miserable in Miami, unable to enjoy the sun or the beaches for thinking about his crew still trapped in German prison camps. He recalled being stuck there: *"I was required to report to a fancy hotel on Miami Beach for two weeks, and all that time itching to get back to work. Why was I allowed to sit in the sun and feed my face while my crew was in a stinking POW camp and likely starving?"*

He desperately wanted to get back to where the action was in Europe and join the effort to free his friends. He constantly badgered his superiors for another combat flying assignment. Thus Cornell used his free time during R & R to study the complicated rules of the Geneva Convention that was keeping him from returning and found a possible way out. A close reading of the agreement revealed that if the enemy territory had been re-taken, then the restriction against returning did not apply:

"Howsomever, if this territory the subject had occupied was retaken by friendly forces, then the rules started all over again. (Comprende vous?) These convoluted rules apparently allowed me to return to Europe anyway."

Since Cornell had evaded in Belgium and France, and these two territories were now in Allied control, he pointed out to anyone who would listen that he was then free to return. He wrote a lengthy request outlining his position and sent it through official channels to Air Force Headquarters in Washington. Reluctantly the brass agreed, and Cornell was assigned to bomber crew training at Drew Army Airfield in Tampa, Florida.

There, Cornell found that the Chief of Training was an old squadron commander from the 100th Bomb Group, "Bucky" Elton, now a Lt. Colonel. Cornell pleaded his case to Elton, who suggested instead that he apply for B-29 training and head to the Far East. Cornell persisted, and was finally given a new crew and got his orders to proceed to Europe. After a few shakedown flights, the crew was soon on its way to Brooklyn, NY. At the shipyards they boarded the Queen Elizabeth II, which because of its speed had been converted to a troop carrier. Speedy was a good description, for in three days he was back in England.

Arriving in London, he learned his new assignment was the 100th Bomb Group again! So it was back to Thorpe-Abbotts. After leading several training flights, Cornell complained about missing the real action and so was put on two of the last combat missions to Far Eastern Europe. Then, even though the war was not yet officially over, Cornell's Group was tasked with another type of mission, delivering food supplies to the starving people of Holland. The winter of 1944 was one of the coldest in recent records and a German embargo of fuel and food to the western Netherlands caused a steep drop in food supplies. Although the Allies had liberated the southern part of the country, the Germans stubbornly held on the to the ports. In addition, as they retreated, they destroyed the docks and bridges and flooded the countryside to impede the progress of the Allies. As a result, famine spread through the countryside, resulting in the deaths of an estimated 18,000 people.

The bomb bays of the B-17s of the 8th Air Force were modified, stripping out the bomb racks, and loaded with food. Cornell and the other pilots flew at near ground level to deliver their cargo: *"This time I was on the other end of the air drop, and I felt awfully good about returning the favor on a small scale, this being just across the Belgian border a short distance from Izegem. Of course I knew firsthand about the near starvation there."*

They found out the modified bomb bays, once fitted with stable platforms, could hold much more than food. So it was that his squadron was given the task of flying out the French survivors of the concentration camps in newly liberated Austria. The first mission called for a survivor pickup at Mauthausen Concentration Camp near Linz, Austria. Mauthausen, constructed near a granite quarry, was first the site of a prison and work camp. Prisoners were from all nations, consisting mostly of Jews and political prisoners. By 1945, more than 20,000 prisoners were transferred from other concentration camps to make a total of over 65,000 inmates, which included 3,179 Frenchmen. Liberated during 4 through 6 May, 1945 by units of the 11th Armored Division of the Patton's Third Army, the American troops found it necessary to try to return many of the released inmates to their home country. For this reason, they called upon airplanes of the 8th Air Force for assistance. Hence the rapid conversion of bombers to transport duty.

For this assignment, Cornell took along just his regular copilot, navigator, and crew chief to leave room for more passengers. Flying into the hastily-constructed landing field with a runway that was just barely adequate, Cornell remembered: *"It sure felt STRANGE to be landing on a kraut field with Stukas still in evidence. These wretched victims were crammed thirty-five Frenchmen at a time and rushed to Paris."*

The survivors were in such poor condition that they were simply dusted with DDT powder and hurriedly placed aboard the modified B-17s. With his plane loaded, Cornell flew straight to the waiting hospitals and physicians in Paris. Cornell thought he knew what the released prisoners would enjoy, so he altered his route to include a flying sweep over the city. When they came in sight of the Eiffel Tower, they shouted and cried so he obligingly circled it several times so even the sick ones could get a look. Cornell recalled the event: *"When we came in sight of the Eiffel Tower, there was much jubilation among my passengers who had long since despaired of ever seeing their beloved Paris again, and believe me there was copious shedding of tears. In sympathy with them, I guess you could include me."*

After they were unloaded at the field hospital, Cornell flew straight back to Mauthausen for a second and third load of survivors. He gave each group the grand air tour of the city before landing. Cornell may have slightly bent the rules on the last air tour, for after his third delivery, he was met at the Operations Shack by a Major who angrily accused him of flying under the Eiffel Tower. Cornell replied that he did not know a B-17 could clear under the tower. He never heard any repercussions, so he forgot about it.

Since the converted B-17 made a fairly good small airliner, Cornell and the other pilots were called upon to make other trips, even to the Gibraltar, Madrid, and North Africa. They also trained other crews with long flights over the North Atlantic.

As the war in Europe ended on 9 May 1945 Cornell was offered the chance to remain in the Air Force, and he always wanted to go to the Pacific Theatre, so he agreed. He was shipped back to the United States, landing at Boston on the day Japan surrendered, August 14, 1945.

Epilog

After The War

Cornell Shaddix - After electing to remain in the Air Force, Cornell served as a B-47 Pilot in the Strategic Air Command (SAC). Upon retiring, he spent a few years near Maxwell AFB in Montgomery, Alabama playing golf, but he longed to return to his home in Winston County. All during his military career, whenever he had a chance to put a few spare dollars together, he would send them to his father with a request to purchase a little more land close to his old home place. His father later told Cornell that he thought the investment was not prudent, since the land in that area was so poor and rocky, but at least it had the advantage of being cheap. But his father complied and over the years Cornell had managed to accumulate over 600 acres of land in an area just west of Double Springs, Alabama. Just about all the land was now in tall timber as pines had replaced the old cropland.

Cornell and his wife Esther returned to his land in the 1970s and built a beautiful home in the middle of the pines. Cornell reconnected with some of his old classmates, including the author's father. They found they both shared a passion for old cars, with my father restoring and rebuilding Model A Fords while Cornell was more interested in the earlier Model T Fords. They began traveling together on their car-hunting expeditions, searching out old barns and swap meets for cars and

parts of cars.   Cornell began poring over automobile
history books and Ford repair manuals to be able to
identify any part that had once belonged to a Model T. He
realized the role of the Ford Model T in putting the nation
on wheels, so he became knowledgeable in every aspect of
the Model T. He would be absolutely delighted when he
was able to find a part and would invariably purchase it
on the spot. He didn't even haggle on the price, mostly
because it was cheap anyway. Before long, he was running
out of space to store the parts, so he built more barns and
sheds to store his purchases. As he found the parts he
would lovingly restore them and put them on shelves or
hang them on the walls. He restored the four-cylinder
engines and stacked them on his workbenches. He rebuilt
Model T wheels by replacing the wooden spokes and hung
them on the barn walls.   Fenders were straightened,
sandblasted, primed, and then painted black—every single
one was painted black.   Other members of the local
antique car club were convinced that Cornell was a "parts-
nut," or one who loved simply collecting parts.

Then one day, he simply quit buying parts and
began assembling cars. Over the next couple of years he
assembled four complete, running and driving Model Ts.
The first completed model was the rarest model, a 1914
"Brass T" which featured, as the description implies, a
brass radiator and brass headlights.   Next was a T
speedster, with a stripped down, racing body, then a
"mother-in-law" version which featured a rear facing
passenger seat, presumably for the mother-in-law.
Finally, he built a depot hack, a sort of wooden-bodied

forerunner of the woody station wagon. Needless to say, he had plenty of spare parts for all the vehicles. He would drive them in local parades and give lectures to anyone who stopped by on the many ingenious features of the Model T Ford design.

Cornell passed away on Jun 30 2007 at the age of 87.

George Sullivan, Copilot - After Sullivan was released from the P.O.W. camp he was returned to the states to rebuild his health. After a period in a military hospital, he left the Army when the war ended and returned to his home in Auburn, New York. He died in 1947 in the crash of an antique biplane that he was piloting.

Cole M. Dailey, Bombardier - When released from the POW camp Dailey returned to the U.S. and began a career in the Army Air Force. When the Air Force was made a separate service in 1947 he chose to stay with the Air Force. In his later military career he served not only in the Korean War, but the Vietnam conflict, making him one of the few to serve in all three wars. Retired as a Lt. Colonel, Dailey died in Oct. 1990 and buried in Arlington National Cemetery, Arlington, VA.

Victor J. Layton, OSS - In 1945 Capt. Layton was awarded the Distinguished Service Cross for *"extraordinary heroism in connection with military operations against an armed enemy while serving with Office of Strategic Services, in action against enemy forces on 21 April 1944 to 12 September 1944. After having been parachuted into France, Captain Layton achieved his mission of organization, arming and training resistance forces with extraordinary courage and ability. Despite a* *large-scale enemy attack which caused the loss of most of the personnel which he had assembled against formidable obstacles, he managed his escape under intense enemy fire, with unabated persistence and coolness, reorganizing his group and led it in numerous successful attacks against the enemy."* Layton remained in the Army Air Force after the war ended and was first stationed in Germany, where he met his wife. He then served in the Air Force during the Korean War and participated in research projects for the Air Force in cold weather testing and building bases in extreme northern areas. He then served in Viet Nam and retired as a Colonel in 1967. He worked on a light twin aircraft project for de Havilland Aircraft in Canada and also worked with several projects to bring water to areas in Africa. After he retired for the second time, he and his wife ran a small inn in New England before they moved to Vermont. He died on Aug. 8th 2010 at the age of 88.

Harry Tennenbaum, Navigator - Left behind in the last mission of Ol' Dad because he had been trained in the newest radar navigation, Tennenbaum was later reassigned to Lt. David G. Raiford's crew as Radar Navigator (Mickey) and completed all his assigned missions before being shipped back to the States.

Jacques Paris de Bollardière, Free French Army, - After his unit was swept up by Patton's Army, Col. Bollardière returned to England, where he then parachuted into Holland. After the war he fought with the French Army in the first Indochina war, and later in the Algerian War. He was promoted to Brigadier General in 1956, at that time the youngest General in the French Army. He resigned from the Army in 1958 in protest of their policies and later became an outspoken pacifist. He passed away in 1986 and was buried in Vannes, Brittany.

Capt. Barry Goldwater, Instructor - After the war ended Goldwater remained active in the Air Force Reserve, eventually retiring as a Command Pilot with the rank of Major General. Over his flying career Goldwater checked out and was certified in 165 types of aircraft, including the B-52. As a Colonel he founded the Arizona Air National Guard and he desegregated it two years before the rest of the US military services. After he returned home to Arizona, Goldwater entered politics, ran for City Council of Phoenix, was elected and went on to be elected Senator five times (1953-1965). He was the Republican Party's nominee for President of the U.S. in 1964, losing to Lyndon B. Johnson.

Curtis LeMay – In 1944, LeMay, then a Colonel, was transferred to the Far East, where he led the XXI Bomber Command in the Pacific. As in Europe, he altered tactics of the B-29 crews to make them more effective. Known for his headstrong methods, as a General LeMay returned to Europe as commander of USAFE and directed the Berlin airlift. He returned to the US to head the Strategic Air Command (SAC) where he became known as an advocate of preemptive Nuclear War. In 1957 he was promoted to the Chief of Staff of the Air Force, where he often disagreed with the policies of other leaders. He retired in 1965, and in 1968 became the running mate of George Wallace in a third party presidential campaign. He died in

1990 and was buried at the Air Force Academy cemetery in Colorado Springs, CO.

Paul Tibbets – After completing 43 missions in Europe, Tibbets was transferred in 1943 back to the states to help work out problems with the new Boeing B-29. He was placed in charge of the 509th Composite Group, which was given the task of dropping an atomic bomb. He piloted the plane, named after his mother Enola Gay, that dropped the first atomic bomb on Hiroshima, Japan on August 6 1945. After tours in Europe, he was promoted to Brigadier General in 1959 and retired in 1966. He passed away in 2007 and in accordance with his wishes his ashes were scattered over the English Channel.

Sumner Reeder, Squadron Commander, - Promoted to Major, Reeder completed 50 missions and was reassigned stateside to transition into C-54s. Unfortunately, he was killed in a training accident in March, 1945 off the coast of Florida while flying out of Homestead AFB.

David R. Talbott, evadee, - After the war Talbott returned to his home state of Maryland where he founded a successful concrete finishing business. In conjunction with this business Talbott invented and patented several concrete finishing machines, which he manufactured and sold.

Jimmy Stewart, Pilot, actor. - After the war Stewart remained active in the Air Force Reserve and was promoted to Brigadier General in 1959. He was qualified to fly the B-47 and the B-52 and retired from the Reserve in 1968. He made his first film after the war in 1946, his third for director Frank Capra, entitled *"It's a Wonderful*

Life," for which he was nominated for an Academy Award. Among his many movies, he starred in several about the Air Force, including *The Glenn Miller Story* in 1954 and *The Strategic Air Command* in 1955. In all, Stewart was nominated for five Academy Awards, winning one for his role in *The Philadelphia Story* and receiving one Lifetime Achievement award.

Sources

Allen, Robert S., *Lucky Forward: The History of Patton's Third U.S. Army*, New York: The Vanguard Press, 1947.

Bradley, Omar, *A Soldier's Story*, New York: Henry Holt and Company, 1951.

Brown, Malcolm, *Spitfire Summer*, London: Carleton Books, 2000.

Bryant, Arthur, *The Turn of the Tide*, New York: Doubleday & Company, 1957.

Collins, Larry and LaPierre, Dominique, *Is Paris Burning?* New York: Simon and Schuster, 1965.

Crosby, Harry H., *A Wing and A Prayer*, New York: Harper Collins, 1993.

Doolittle, James H. "Jimmy", *I Could Never Be So Lucky Again*, New York: Bantam Books, 1991.

Jablonsky, Edward, *Flying Fortress*, New York: Doubleday & Company, 1965.

———, *Air War: Outraged Skies and Wings of Fire*, New York: Doubleday & Company, 1971.

Lawson, Don, *The French Resistance,* New York: Simon & Schuster, 1984.

LeMay, Curtis W. with Kantor, MacKinlay, *Mission with LeMay: My Story*, New York: Doubleday & Company, 1965.

McGuire, Melvin W. and Hadley, Robert, *Bloody Skies,* Las Cruces, NM: Yucca Tree Press, 1993.

Morgan, Robert C. and Power, Ron, *The Man Who Flew the Memphis Belle*, New York: The Penguin Group, 2001.

O'Donnell, Patrick K., *Operatives, Spies and Saboteurs*, New York: Simon & Schuster, 2004.

Perry, Mark, *Partners in Command: George Marshall and Dwight Eisenhower in War and Peace*, New York: Penguin Books, 2007.

Persico, Joseph E., *Piercing the Reich*, New York: Ballantine Books, 1979.

Pogue, Forrest C., *George C. Marshall: Ordeal and Hope*, New York: The Viking Press, 1965.

Probert, Henry, *Bomber Harris, His life and Times*, London: Greenhill Books, 2001.

Shaddix, Winans Cornell, *What? The Bloody Hundredth Again?*, Privately published, 1997.

Simmons, Kenneth W., *Kriege*, New York: Thomas Nelson & Sons, 1960.

Speer, Albert, *Inside the Third Reich*, New York: Bonanza Books, 1970.

Winterbottom, F.M., *The Ultra Secret*, New York: The Dell Publishing Company, 1974.

Index

www.ingramcontent.com/pod-product-compliance
Lightning Source LLC
La Vergne TN
LVHW011227080426
835509LV00005B/354

* 9 780578 151274 *